HAPPY BABY, HEALTHY MOM

PREGNANCY JOURNAL

BY ROBERT A. GREENE, M.D., AND LAURIE TARKAN, WITH MORGAN PRITCHARD, R.N.

POTTER STY

D1401022

Published in the United States by Clarkson Potter/
Publishers, an imprint of the Crown Publishing Group,
a division of Random House, Inc., New York.
Potter Style is a trademark and Potter and colophon
are registered trademarks of Random House, Inc.

ISBN: 978-0-307-38221-4

Printed in China

Design by Robin Terra

10 9 8 7 6 5 4 3 2 1

FIRST EDITION

introduction

Journaling Your Way Through
A Healthy, Happy Pregnancy

With this journal, you are embarking on a personal journey just for yourself. There is the public you—a glowing mom-to-be, ecstatic about your pregnancy, round and getting rounder. But there is also the private you—about to cross the threshold into the world of parenthood, already feeling protective pangs toward your child, perhaps feeling nauseous or tired, or having mixed emotions about your pregnancy. This journal is for the private you. It's a place where you can experience the joy, the excitement, and the fun of being pregnant, but also a safe place for you to put some of your concerns or less than cheery thoughts on paper.

This book is one part writing journal and one part guide for maintaining a healthy lifestyle. Writing may be your path to a peaceful, stress-free, and healthy pregnancy. Journaling can be incredibly helpful in not only capturing your joy, but in relieving your concerns, reducing your stress, and keeping track of all your medical details, and in doing so, improving how you feel mentally and physically while you're pregnant and through the postpartum months that follow childbirth.

You and your baby will also benefit from the tips, facts, questionnaires, suggested questions to ask your doctor, and the prompts for journaling. All the recommendations in the journal—the diet and lifestyle advice, the many tips for relieving symptoms, the do-it-yourself questionnaires and in-office tests to take with your doctor—are all drawn from the *Perfect Hormone Balance for Pregnancy Program*. This program is based on cutting-edge research on hormones and how they can impact your pregnancy—for better or worse.

3

Dr. Greene is a reproductive endocrinologist and obstetrician and gynecologist with years of research into the brain, hormones, and how they affect our symptoms and our health. Dr. Greene's program aims to reduce your consumption of unhealthy foods, like simple sugars and unhealthy fats, increase your exercise, lower stress, and avoid harmful chemicals in the environment as well as in your home, your cosmetics, your food, and water. All these elements can affect your developing baby. Your goal is to increase the good ones and decrease the harmful ones to have the healthiest pregnancy and the healthiest, happiest baby you can.

One of Dr. Greene's key tenets is that *symptoms matter.* While your doctor and your well-meaning friends may send you the message to grin and bear your symptoms, studies have found that *not* managing your symptoms, including morning sickness, can lead to problems during your pregnancy. This journal provides the space and opportunity to keep track of your symptoms through questionnaires that are modified from standard medical scales used by physicians. You can bring your results to your doctor to show her that your symptoms are legitimate and they should be addressed. Throughout the journal, there's advice about safe ways to prevent and relieve symptoms of pregnancy. If you want more detailed explanations and more treatment options, refer to *Dr. Greene's Perfect Hormone Balance for Pregnancy.*

An essential aspect of having a healthy pregnancy and a healthy baby is minimizing stress and reducing stress hormones that can reach your baby and affect its development. Studies have shown that stress hormones can pass through the placenta, the sac that nourishes the baby, and negatively impact the pregnancy. Lowering your stress hormones can lower your risk of pregnancy complications, and also greatly reduce your risk of depression and anxiety during pregnancy and the postpartum period. Journaling has been shown to be an effective way to reduce stress and manage emotions.

Most pregnant women don't have time or energy to write at length each day. This weekly journal offers different types of opportunities for journaling: a series of questions or thoughts to respond to in a paragraph or two, a single question to answer at length, an opportunity to write a letter to your developing child, and space for freewriting—essentially free-associating on paper as a way of accessing thoughts you may not know you have. Freewriting is a great entry into journaling for those with little experience. You simply write without stopping, without thinking too hard, without judging yourself, but writing whatever comes to mind, even if you write "I don't know what to write" until you fill a page. You don't ever have to share this journal with anyone, so write freely.

In our hectic lives, it's easy to buzz through the day, not stopping and thinking much about how we feel, both physically and mentally. This journal is an easy reminder to take a moment to enjoy being pregnant and think about the future life with your baby. And it will also be a cherished reminder of your intimate feelings during your pregnancy.

FIRST TRIMESTER

weeks **1** *to* **13**

AFTER YOU'VE REVELED IN
the news of your pregnancy, you'll
likely want to start gathering information about what you need to do to
keep your baby healthy. During the first trimester,
your body is geared toward protecting your developing
baby, and providing the nutrients necessary for these
early stages of development. The baby—now called
an embryo—needs your greatest care and protection.
It is during these early weeks that all of its organs are
forming and cells are rapidly dividing. The fast
turnover of cells makes them more susceptible to
damage. Some evolutionary experts believe morning
sickness is a mechanism developed to protect the
embryo from potent but naturally occurring chemicals
in our food. You can help protect your baby from less >

natural chemicals that are in conventionally grown foods, from man-made fats like trans fats, and from the chemical by-products of overeating, as well as from stress hormones. Many of these chemicals can pass through the placenta and affect the baby's development.

The first trimester may test your mettle. Depending on how severe your fatigue and morning sickness are, you may be counting the days until the end of this trimester, when you will begin to feel like yourself again. But rather than endure your symptoms, it's better for you, your pregnancy, and your baby's development to try to treat any symptoms you have, including morning sickness, to keep them from worsening and causing other problems down the road.

week

1

SPECIAL NOTE: Your pregnancy began with the first day of your last menstrual period. Since fertilization actually takes place around the end of the third week of your cycle, it is likely that you are well beyond the first week of your pregnancy when you start this journal. Regardless of where you are, begin here and read the recommendations for diet and lifestyle changes as well as for symptom relief; this advice builds from week to week, with the foundation being set in the earliest weeks. Take this opportunity to reflect back on how you felt when you first realized you were pregnant, but don't worry about catching up with your journaling all in one sitting or it may feel like homework.

Pregnancy Pointer Once you find out you're pregnant, one of the first things you should do is start taking a prescription prenatal vitamin. These multivitamins geared specifically to the nutritional needs of pregnant women have been found to reduce the risk of birth defects and pregnancy complications. Ask your doctor to prescribe one over the phone so you don't have to wait until your first appointment. Prescription prenatal vitamins are not all alike, but some comprehensive vitamins that will meet most of your dietary needs for a healthy pregnancy are Natelle Prefer, PrimaCare, Citracal, Duet Tablets, or Optinate.

Healthy Eating for Two

More and more people are buying organic food as it becomes readily available in supermarkets and superstores. Now that you're eating for you and your developing baby, it's the perfect time to jump on this organic bandwagon if you haven't already. Conventionally grown foods contain many food additives, pesticides, herbicides, and antibiotics that may harm a developing embryo. Some of these chemicals are hormone disrupters, which change the way your natural hormones function, and can potentially impact the development of the baby's brain. Try not to worry if you don't become a health food junkie overnight. But as you shop, start to be aware of the range of organic options at the store and begin to choose organic when you can. By substituting organic products whenever possible, you can reduce your exposure to these substances by about 90 percent.

Record your starting weight _Monday July 6 2009   170 lbs._

Calculating Your Due Date Your due date is an estimate. For most pregnancies, nobody knows the actual date of fertilization and how long it took your embryo to reach the uterus. That's why only 5 percent of women deliver exactly on their due date. To calculate your due date, begin with the first day of your last menstrual cycle and count nine months forward, then add seven days. For example. If your last period started on May 1, adding nine months brings you to February 1, plus seven days gives you a due date of February 8.

The first day of your last menstrual cycle _____

+ nine months + seven days = your due date _____

Baby Milestones

The first week of your pregnancy actually began with the first day of your last menstrual cycle. During this time one of your eggs was being primed for ovulation, a process that began two months ago when a group of immature eggs, called follicles, began to mature. Follicles begin with twenty-three pairs of chromosomes, which carry your genetic code in the form of DNA. When follicles mature, they drop one chromosome from every pair to make room for the incoming twenty-three carried by your husband's sperm. When sperm fertilizes egg, twenty-three original pairs of chromosomes are formed, creating your unique baby.

Journaling

Date _____

A safe place to let your thoughts flow without stopping, thinking too hard, or judging yourself.

Were you trying to get pregnant? For how long?

_____

_____

_____

_____

_____

_____

_____

_____

_____

_____

_____

_____

Was there anything special about the day you conceived?
Were you on vacation or a "date night," was it a less romantic
attempt to conceive, or was it an unplanned roll in the hay?

_____

_____

_____

_____

_____

How and when did you find out you were pregnant and who was with you?

_____

_____

_____

_____

_____

week

Pregnancy Pointer Exercise has many benefits for you and your baby—it keeps your metabolism active, improves circulation, tones your muscles, minimizes excessive weight gain, and keeps stress hormones in check. Aim for 30 to 45 minutes of moderate exercise five days a week. Don't beat yourself up if you don't achieve this each week—there will be weeks that it will be harder to motivate yourself—and any efforts to be active will benefit your pregnancy. If you were not exercising before you became pregnant, consult your healthcare provider. Use the weekly Keeping Fit logs in this journal to track your exercise habits.

Healthy Eating for Two Try not to increase your calories just yet. During the first trimester, the embryo is evolving into a fetus and forming its organs. It is building a foundation, but growing very little in size, and does not need a great deal of energy to thrive. You won't need to increase your calorie intake until the second trimester. In fact, if you gain more than three to four pounds in the first twelve weeks of your pregnancy, you may be on course for excessive weight gain. The exception to this rule is if you were underweight before conceiving.

Important Herbal supplements are not well studied in pregnant women and the dietary supplement industry is unregulated. Some pills may not contain the specified amount of a nutrient, or worse, they might be tainted with toxins and pollutants. Taking these supplements are an unnecessary risk. Consult your healthcare provider before continuing or starting herbal or other high dose supplements.

Stress Relief Tip There are many ways to achieve relaxation and lower your stress hormones, but yoga has been the most studied relaxation practice. It improves blood flow to the placenta and reduces the amount of stress hormones that reach your baby. If you're experienced at yoga, practice it at home for about 20 to 30 minutes, five days a week, or aim for taking a 45- to 60-minute class twice a week. Tell your instructor that you're pregnant. If you are new to the practice, take a beginner yoga class—it's better to learn yoga under the guidance of an instructor—and start out gradually.

Baby Milestones

During this week, one immature egg, or follicle, rises above the rest, and in an act of domination, produces hormones that suppress the growth of all other follicles.

When mature, the dominant follicle sends a hormonal message to your brain to trigger ovulation. Typically, ovulation takes only minutes, and the egg is quickly fertilized by your partner's sperm at the beginning of the fallopian tube.

Keeping Fit Aim for five 30- to 45-minute sessions a week—remember, don't beat yourself up if you can't reach this goal. Fill in the circles with the number of minutes that you spend exercising each day.

ACTIVITY	MONDAY	TUESDAY	WEDNESDAY	THURSDAY	FRIDAY	SATURDAY	SUNDAY
walking/ aerobic exercise							
yoga/ stretching							
strength training							

Journaling

Date _____

Freewrite on the following pages, writing whatever comes to mind, even if it doesn't make sense.

_____

_____

_____

_____

week 3

Pregnancy Pointer It's important to begin your healthy pregnancy lifestyle as soon as you can, but some doctors ask you to wait a month or two for your first prenatal visit. To avoid this "pregnant pause," request an earlier appointment to discuss your health, diet, exercise, and other important lifestyle changes.

Important Many of the chemicals in pesticides and herbicides can cross the placenta, exposing your baby to these potentially damaging chemicals. Try to reduce avoidable exposure to these toxins. Wash fresh produce before eating it, don't apply pesticides indoors, and avoid using fungicides, herbicides, and pesticides in your lawn and garden while pregnant.

Stress Relief Tip One of the first lifestyle changes many women make is giving up coffee or tea. But going cold turkey on caffeine can temporarily raise stress hormones that cross the placenta, and have a negative impact on your baby's development. The fact is, studies have shown that pregnant women who drink coffee in moderation (fewer than eight 8-ounce cups a day) do not have an increased risk of complications, nor do their babies have an increased risk of developmental or other problems. Coffee is also one of the richest sources of dietary antioxidants, an important nutrient that protects you and your baby from free radicals, highly reactive chemicals that can damage cells. To be cautious limit yourself to no more than three 8-ounce cups a day, and if you want to cut caffeine out altogether, wean yourself off of it slowly to avoid the spike in stress hormones.

Baby Milestones

After your egg and your partner's sperm unite to form a single cell, called a "zygote," it travels the rest of the way through the fallopian tube toward your uterus.

During the journey, it divides approximately every 15 to 24 hours into smaller cells—one cell becomes two, two become four, four become eight and so on, forming a multicell blastocyst that prepares to be implanted into your uterus.

Keeping Fit

Aim for five 30- to 45-minute sessions a week.

ACTIVITY	MONDAY	TUESDAY	WEDNESDAY	THURSDAY	FRIDAY	SATURDAY	SUNDAY
walking/ aerobic exercise							
yoga/ stretching							
strength training							

Journaling

Date _____

Write down your thoughts about the type of healthcare provider you want—a physician, midwife, man or woman, group or sole practitioner, and why?

_____

_____

_____

_____

_____

_____

_____

_____

_____

_____

week 4

Pregnancy Pointer If you are pregnant during flu season (November through March) you should get a flu vaccination. It does not contain a live virus and poses no risk to you or your developing baby. Don't take the nasal spray version, which contains a live virus. Getting a bad flu though does come with risks to the baby. An added benefit: Infants up to one year of age have fewer ear infections if their moms were vaccinated during pregnancy.

Healthy Eating for Two Carbohydrates are the most important fuel source for your developing baby. Try to increase the complex carbohydrates such as fruits, vegetables, and whole grains in your diet, and lower your intake of simple carbohydrates like white breads, pasta, and sweets. Simple carbs are quickly broken down and can cause sharp spikes and dips in blood sugar and insulin levels, increasing your risk of gestational diabetes, too much weight gain, and having a large baby.

Symptom Soother: Fatigue You can thank your rising levels of the hormone progesterone for the intense fatigue you may feel and for "pregnancy brain," a forgetfulness that occurs in expectant moms. Progesterone, which rises steadily, is essential for keeping the embryo securely attached to your uterus and preventing miscarriage. To fend off the fog of fatigue, take 15- to 20-minute catnaps (longer naps can make you feel more groggy when you awake). Also consider taking a brisk 10-minute walk to get your blood flowing to your brain.

Sleep Questionnaire
Your hormones may be making you feel groggy, but you may not be getting enough sleep as well. Take the Pregnancy Sleep Risk Assessment on page 196 to make sure you're not sleep deprived. Record your results there so you can compare them to how you feel later in the pregnancy. Take the assessment about once a month.

Baby Milestones

Nested safely in your womb, the cluster of cells that is called a blastocyst separates into two parts, with one eventually becoming your baby and the other forming the placenta and umbilical cord—the lifeline that carries blood and nutrients from the placenta to your baby and removes its waste products. By the end of this week the yolk sac, which contains the baby's first red blood cells, is fully developed. The amniotic sac that surrounds the embryo is now fully formed. You are officially pregnant (congratulations!).

Stress Relief Tip It's normal to have some jitters during your first prenatal visit. Take your partner or friend or family member with you. Bring a list of questions so you don't forget anything, and don't be afraid to ask for clear explanations if you don't understand something.

Keeping Fit Aim for five 30- to 45-minute sessions a week.

ACTIVITY	MONDAY 7/6	TUESDAY 7/7	WEDNESDAY 7/8	THURSDAY 7/9	FRIDAY 7/10	SATURDAY 7/11	SUNDAY 7/12
walking/ aerobic exercise	30min		45min		30min	35min	
yoga/ stretching							
strength training							

Journaling

This may be the week you find out you're pregnant. Describe your emotions.

Excited, releved, ecstatic, nervous,

Describe any concerns or mixed emotions you're feeling now.

We heard from Dr. Stambaugh that my hcg levels more than doubled which means things are going well so far!
Happy the spotting has stopped and hope + the cramps stay away

18

Describe how you feel . . . energetic, tired, hungry, or nauseous.

Tired, emotional,

YOUR FIRST PRENATAL VISIT is the most exciting, as you will confirm the pregnancy with a blood test or ultrasound (the ultrasound can be done as early as week six). Your healthcare provider will also estimate your due date. You probably want to bring your partner as a support person; you'll have a lot of questions and he can help you remember everything you discuss. Be prepared to provide your medical and reproductive history, the date of your last period, and your family medical history. Your doctor might ask about your partner's medical history as well. Be sure to bring a list of medications or supplements you are currently taking. You will have a physical exam including a pelvic exam and a Pap smear if indicated, as well as routine blood tests, and you'll be asked to provide a urine sample. Take a list of questions or concerns with you and discuss them with your healthcare provider.

Here are some suggested questions to ask your practitioner:

Will I always see the same healthcare provider during my visits?

Who will deliver my baby if you are not available?

At which hospitals or birthing centers do you have privileges?

What level of exercise is safe for me?

If I've had a cesarean delivery, is VBAC (vaginal birth after cesarean) an option for me?

How many ultrasounds will I have?

Should I take an iron supplement with my prenatal vitamin?

If you're seeing a midwife: What doctors do you work with?

19

Notes for this **Prenatal Visit**   Date _____

SYMPTOMS Write down any symptoms you have to discuss with your doctor, and then describe her response.

Symptoms

MD's response

_____   _____

_____   _____

_____   _____

_____   _____

Health Measures

The following tests should be part of your first trimester care. Not all these tests are necessary for each woman and they don't all need to be performed on your first visit. If your healthcare provider performs any of these during this visit, record your health measures here. You will also have a blood test in the first trimester that's a comprehensive screen for health problems and various viruses such as hepatitis B or HIV.

YOUR RESULTS

Your estimated due date _____

Your weight _____

Blood pressure _____

Urine test for sugar*   yes   no
*indicates gestational diabetes or other metabolic problems

Urine test for protein*   yes   no
*indicates a bladder infection or onset of preeclampsia

Blood type (circle one)   A   B   AB   O

Rh factor (circle one)   Rh-negative   Rh-positive

Additional Tests to Request

Several hormones are critical for maintaining a pregnancy and for the health of your baby. Their level can indicate a healthy pregnancy or a potential problem. Testing for these four hormones are not part of the routine prenatal exam, but if performed early enough, tests can help predict and prevent early complications. THYROID imbalances often go undiagnosed, but if left untreated, may lead to miscarriage or to developmental delays in children. *Test: Complete thyroid panel.* The hormone PROGESTERONE encourages blood flow to your uterus, necessary for creating a healthy home for the embryo. If progesterone doesn't rise adequately, the pregnancy will be threatened. *Test: Serum progesterone.* HUMAN CHORIONIC GONADOTROPIN, or HCG, is critical because it triggers your ovaries to produce progesterone. *Test: Quantitative HCG.* GLYCOSYLATED HEMOGLOBIN OR HEMOGLOBIN-A1C measures your average blood sugar level, a signpost for gestational diabetes or high insulin levels.

TEST RESULTS

Test   Result

Complete thyroid panel   _____

Serum progesterone   _____

Quantitative HCG   _____

Glycosylated hemoglobin (HgA1c)   _____

Notes After This Visit

Describe your thoughts about your visit or any important
points your doctor made:

_____

_____

_____

_____

_____

_____

_____

_____

_____

_____

_____

_____

_____

_____

_____

_____

week 5

Pregnancy Pointer Try to schedule a routine dental exam now, and tell your dentist you're pregnant. Untreated infection or inflammation at the base of your teeth increases the risk of preterm birth by more than two and half times. Ask your partner to get his dental exam too. Bacteria in his saliva that causes gum disease and cavities can easily be passed to you.

Flexitarian Tip Consider adopting a Flexitarian (flexible + vegetarian) diet, essentially a diet that relies more on plant-based foods than animal-based foods. Plant foods (grains, fruits, and vegetables) are rich in nutrients and high in fiber and water, making them healthy, filling, and satisfying. Plant proteins like beans, nuts, and lentils are healthier protein sources than animal, fish, and fowl because they contain fewer toxins. While pregnant you need between 75 and 100 grams of protein a day, about double what you need when you're eating for one. Increase your plant proteins to reach this goal. At least 75 percent of your daily diet should come from plant foods, the remaining 25 percent can come from animal products (meat, fish, poultry, and dairy foods).

22

Baby Milestones

The embryo now looks like a flattened disk made up of three layers of tissue that will ultimately form into specific cells and organs. The neural tube is forming and will develop into the brain and spinal cord. Blood cells are beginning to emerge from the yolk sac, and cells begin to form two heart tubes that will soon connect with the rudimentary circulatory system.

Stress Relief Tip During pregnancy, dreams can be incredibly vivid and intense. As dreams are a profound reflection of your feelings—joy, anxiety, and stress—especially regarding major life changes, it could be eye-opening to write them down in the morning and think about their meaning. Dreams during the first trimester often involve swimming, botanical themes, your childhood, small buildings, heavy luggage, or giving birth to a full-grown child.

Keeping Fit Aim for five 30- to 45-minute sessions a week.

ACTIVITY	MONDAY	TUESDAY	WEDNESDAY	THURSDAY	FRIDAY	SATURDAY	SUNDAY
walking/ aerobic exercise							
yoga/ stretching							
strength training							

Important Avoid low-carbohydrate fad diets. Carbohydrates provide nutrients like folic acid and glucose that are critical for healthy brain and spinal cord development of your baby.

23

Journaling   Date _____

If you've been to your first visit, describe your feelings about your healthcare provider.

_____

_____

_____

_____

_____

_____

_____

What are your thoughts about when you will tell family, friends, and your employer that you're pregnant.

_____

_____

_____

_____

_____

_____

_____

_____

Describe your prepregnancy eating habits and whether there is anything you'd like to change.

_____

_____

_____

_____

_____

_____

_____

_____

_____

_____

_____

_____

_____

week 6

Pregnancy Pointer Exercising will feel like the last thing you want to do if you have morning sickness, but it can boost your energy and help fight the fatigue of pregnancy. Try to walk for at least 30 minutes at a "conversational pace" five days a week. If you can't do it all at once, split it up into 10-minute intervals. It's best to exercise before noon, even if you're getting it by "activating" your lifestyle, like taking the stairs, picking up your pace when walking around, parking farther away from your office, or walking to do your errands.

Symptom Soother: Morning Sickness

Up to 80 percent of pregnant women suffer from morning sickness (yes, a lucky minority escape it). The hormone HCG (human chorionic gonadotropin) is likely the main culprit; morning sickness develops as levels of HCG begin to rise, and subsides as HCG diminishes around the thirteenth week of pregnancy. To reduce morning sickness, avoid big meals, rise slowly when you get out of bed, carry a lemon in your purse to chase away nauseating odors, and try acupressure on your wrist with Sea-Bands, used for seasickness.

Healthy Eating for Two

If you cook with gourmet salts, like sea salt or kosher salt, make sure it's iodized. You need 35 percent more iodine when pregnant, but most pregnant women don't get enough, potentially contributing to thyroid issues and fatigue. During pregnancy you need a shake more than half a teaspoon of iodized salt a day.

Morning Sickness Questionnaire

If you're feeling nauseous or are vomiting, complete the Morning Sickness Questionnaire on page 197 and record your results. Talk to your doctor about your symptoms and treatments if your scores are high. Take this test twice a week as your symptoms persist.

Baby Milestones

The chest cavity is forming around your baby's rudimentary lungs and heart—his heart now begins to beat and the rhythmic movement can be seen on an ultrasound. His eyes and ears and limbs are beginning to form.

Important Tap water often contains unhealthy levels of compounds that may be harmful to your baby. Invest in a water filter for your primary sink; a reverse osmosis filter removes chlorine, mercury, lead, cadmium, benzene, asbestos, pesticides, and pipe sediments.

Keeping Fit Aim for five 30- to 45-minute sessions a week

ACTIVITY	MONDAY	TUESDAY	WEDNESDAY	THURSDAY	FRIDAY	SATURDAY	SUNDAY
walking/ aerobic exercise							
yoga/ stretching							
strength training							

Journaling

Date _____

Freewrite about anything that comes to mind.

_____

_____

week 7

Pregnancy Pointer You may have already received compliments about your pregnant glow. The flush is caused by a rise in two essential pregnancy hormones. Estradiol (your body's most potent form of estrogen) improves blood flow to your skin, making it pinker; progesterone raises your body temperature as much as two degrees, causing you to perspire more and giving your complexion a hint of shine.

Healthy Eating for Two

Adding fiber to your diet can help avert many potential pregnancy problems like constipation and excess weight gain. It also improves the absorption of other nutrients, allowing you to reap the most benefit from your food. Plus it's essentially calorie-free and won't add to unnecessary weight gain. Start slowly replacing low fiber foods with high fiber alternatives. Your goal is 30 grams a day (you'll have a fiber check-in during week 9).

Five Fiber Boosters:

1. Eat a handful of raisins or dried plums (3 grams of fiber per serving)
2. Switch from white to brown rice (doubles the fiber)
3. Add chickpeas or beans to salad (8 to 12 grams per half serving)
4. Eat unsweetened bran cereal (10 to 14 grams per serving)
5. Eat five servings of fruits and vegetables.

Baby Milestones

Your baby's growth occurs from the head downward. Her eyes, ears and nose are developing, and the esophagus begins to form in preparation for swallowing. Her arm buds have elongated and leg buds now appear. The rapidly developing brain organizes into the forebrain, mid-brain, and hindbrain, and the hypothalamus (the processing center for hormones and regulating center of our basic functions) begins to form. By the end of this week, the top of the neural tube will close to protect the developing spinal cord. The length of the embryo can now be measured from the crown (top of the head) to the rump. By now the crown-rump length is 3 to 5 mm—about the length of a pencil tip.

 **Symptom Soother: Bleeding** If you're experiencing spotting or bleeding, call your healthcare provider. Bleeding indicates that there has been some separation of the placenta from the uterus, though in many cases, the placenta recovers on its own. Request an ultrasound, as there are certain measures of the gestational sac, your cervix, and other factors that can provide reassuring information that a miscarriage is not imminent. Also request the following tests that measure levels of the key hormones involved in sustaining a pregnancy: progesterone, human chorionic gonadotropin, and thyroid hormone.

Reminder

☐ Morning Sickness Questionnaire: page 197. Take twice this week and talk to your doctor about your symptoms and treatments if your scores are high.

Keeping Fit Aim for five 30- to 45-minute sessions a week.

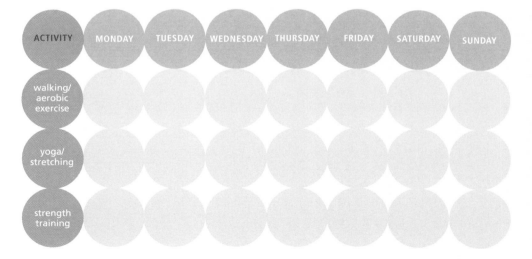

ACTIVITY	MONDAY	TUESDAY	WEDNESDAY	THURSDAY	FRIDAY	SATURDAY	SUNDAY
walking/ aerobic exercise							
yoga/ stretching							
strength training							

Journaling

Date _____

If you have morning sickness or fatigue, describe what your symptoms are like.

_____

_____

_____

_____

_____

What strategies or treatments have you tried in order to lessen
or cope with your morning sickness?

_____

_____

_____

_____

_____

_____

Describe what it has been like to exercise (or not) during this trimester.

_____

_____

_____

_____

_____

_____

week 8

Healthy Eating for Two The nutrients below are essential for a healthy pregnancy. Try to get them through your diet or supplements.

CALCIUM. If you have too little calcium in your bloodstream, your body breaks down your bones in order to provide essential calcium to your baby, resulting in bone loss for you. Get at least 1,300 mg a day through milk and other dairy products, soy foods, and fortified juices and cereals. If you're taking a calcium supplement, take it at bedtime for optimum absorption.

MAGNESIUM. Low levels of magnesium put you at risk for leg cramps, constipation, and preterm labor. You need at least 400 mg a day. Good food sources include whole grains, wheat germ, nuts, green leafy vegetables, broccoli, and bananas. Your prenatal vitamin and calcium supplement with magnesium can fulfill the rest.

VITAMIN C. This antioxidant builds strong bones and teeth and maintains the integrity of connective tissue. Get at least 70 mg a day through citrus fruits, green and red peppers, tomatoes, and kiwi fruit.

IRON. This mineral is a key component of hemoglobin, the protein in red blood cells that transports oxygen throughout your and your baby's body. Too little iron causes fatigue, suppresses your immunity, and increases the risk of miscarriage. A Flexitarian diet, high in beans, whole grains, and dark leafy vegetables, should provide enough iron. If your doctor recommends a supplement, avoid taking it with your calcium since the two minerals compete for absorption.

Pregnancy Pointer If you are struggling to get through the day, try these fatigue-fighting snacks.

> Bananas   > Low fat trail mix
> Dried prunes or cherries   > Raisins
> Almonds   > Oranges

Stress Relief Tip If you're spotting, bleeding, or otherwise worried about miscarriage, stress can have a snowball effect. When stress hormones rise, so too does your risk of miscarriage. Try long-lasting stress-reducing practices such as meditation, biofeedback, or psychotherapy.

Reminder

❏ **Morning Sickness Questionnaire:** page 197. Take twice this week if you're suffering from morning sickness. Talk to your doctor about your symptoms and treatments if your scores are high.

❏ **Sleep Questionnaire:** If you're feeling tired, take the Pregnancy Sleep Risk Assessment on page 196 to make sure you're not sleep deprived.

Baby Milestones

Specialized areas of the brain are beginning to develop. The *cerebellum* coordinates muscular movement, and the *pituitary gland* regulates many hormone functions. The *olfactory bulb,* responsible for your baby's sense of smell, is also forming. Baby teeth are developing and the upper lip begins to take shape.

Stress Relief Tip Nausea can put a damper on romantic thoughts and your sex life. Since nausea is often triggered by smell, try placing pleasant-smelling candles or essential oil diffusers in your home. If your partner wears cologne that now bothers you, ask him to put it away. If rapid movement during sex makes you green around the gills, slow your pace accordingly. And if your schedules allow, try to change the time of day you have sex to a time when your nausea has ebbed.

32

Keeping Fit Aim for five 30- to 45-minute sessions a week.

ACTIVITY	MONDAY	TUESDAY	WEDNESDAY	THURSDAY	FRIDAY	SATURDAY	SUNDAY
walking/ aerobic exercise							
yoga/ stretching							
strength training							

Journaling

Date _____

Describe your new relationship with food (have you had food aversions, cravings, have you been too nauseous to eat, or do you find yourself wolfing down your food because you're famished)?

_____

_____

_____

_____

_____

_____

_____

_____

_____

_____

_____

_____

_____

_____

_____

_____

_____

_____

_____

_____

_____

_____

week 9

Flexitarian Tip To reduce the amount of animal-based protein you eat, divide proportions on your plate so that vegetables, legumes, fruits, and whole grains account for at least two-thirds of the plate, and meat covers less than one-third.

Fiber check-in

What high fiber foods have you increased in your diet? This week, track your fiber intake for three days, listing all your high fiber foods (refer to week 7 for replacement suggestions). If you are getting less than 30 grams a day, consider taking a fiber supplement like Benefiber or FiberChoice.

Day 1 _____

Day 2 _____

Day 3 _____

Symptom Soother: Migraines If you are a migraine sufferer, your rising estradiol levels will most likely minimize your headaches while you're pregnant. To reduce your chance of migraines further, avoid foods that you know trigger an attack, eat foods rich in magnesium (whole grains, wheat germ, nuts, green leafy vegetables, broccoli, and bananas), be sure to stick to a regular routine of meals, exercise, and a consistent sleep schedule.

! **Important** Many fish contain high levels of mercury, which has been linked to brain damage. Fish having the highest amounts of mercury include albacore tuna, shark, swordfish, king mackerel, and tilefish. Some low-mercury fish and seafood options are shrimp, canned light tuna, wild salmon, pollock, and catfish. But to be safe, consider seafood a luxury and consume it rarely. To get the health benefits of essential fatty acids, take a plant-based supplement like Expecta LIPIL, which is safe to take during pregnancy.

Mood Questionnaire

Many physicians do not screen for depression as part of routine prenatal care, yet depression occurs in 10 to 20 percent of pregnant women and has known risks to the mother and her developing baby. Complete the Mood Questionnaire on page 198 and record your score. If your scores are high, speak to your doctor about treatment options. Take this questionnaire at least once every four to six weeks during your pregnancy and through your postpartum period. Seek help if your scores are rising and your symptoms are getting worse.

Reminder
☐ **Morning Sickness Questionnaire: page 197.** Take twice this week and talk to your doctor about your symptoms and treatments if your scores are high.

Baby Milestones
The brain is now developing an astounding 250,000 nerve cells per minute. This week your baby's tongue starts to develop, his ear canals are present, and his eyes are structurally complete, though not yet functioning. Your baby's fingers and thumbs are now formed, but remain webbed.

Keeping Fit Aim for five 30- to 45-minute sessions a week.

ACTIVITY	MONDAY	TUESDAY	WEDNESDAY	THURSDAY	FRIDAY	SATURDAY	SUNDAY
walking/ aerobic exercise							
yoga/ stretching							
strength training							

Journaling

Reflect on what type of parents you can imagine you
and your partner will be and how you visualize your family life.

_____

_____

_____

_____

_____

_____

_____

_____

_____

_____

_____

_____

_____

_____

_____

_____

_____

_____

_____

_____

_____

_____

_____

DURING THIS AND MOST EXAMS in the first and second trimester, you will probably provide a urine sample and have your blood pressure tested and your weight recorded. Take this opportunity to ask any questions you forgot or didn't have time for in your first visit. Write questions down and try to ask them first thing so you don't forget. Make a note of how you are scoring on your questionnaires and discuss any results that concern you with your health-care provider.

Here are some suggested questions to ask your practitioner:

Is there any finding in our family history that is of concern?

What types of concerns or symptoms should I call you about?

Does my job present a risk to my pregnancy and if so, what should I do differently?

Are there any home cleaning products I should avoid?

Are there any vaccinations that I should get?

Was my pap smear normal (if done during last visit)? How were my other test results?

Can I e-mail questions to you between visits?

Notes for this **Prenatal Visit**   Date _____

SYMPTOMS Write down any symptoms you have to discuss with your doctor, and then describe her response.

Symptoms   MD's response

_____   _____

_____   _____

_____   _____

_____   _____

_____   _____

Screening Tests

Your physician may recommend first trimester screening for birth defects or genetic disorders. No single test can detect your risk but screening tests can identify you as low risk or high risk for a potential problem. If you're identified as high risk, you will go on to have a diagnostic test like an **amniocentesis** or ultrasound. When performed between the tenth and fourteenth week, first trimester screening detects about 75 percent of cases of Down's syndrome and birth defects of the abdomen, spine, or heart. It involves a blood test for three hormones—human chorionic gonadotropin (HCG), estriol, and pregnancy-associated plasma protein-A (PAPP-A)—combined with an ultrasound called **nuchal translucency screening** to measure the thickness of the tissue on the back of your baby's neck.

YOUR RESULTS

Your estimated due date _____

Your weight _____

Blood pressure _____

Urine test for sugar _____

Urine test for protein _____

Notes After This Visit

Describe your thoughts about your visit or any important points your doctor made:

_____

_____

_____

_____

_____

_____

_____

_____

week 10

Pregnancy Pointer

You may notice that your sense of smell has become extra sensitive—another symptom of rising estradiol levels. The smell–taste bud connection may also be behind some of your cravings. A heightened sense of smell enhances your ability to taste bitterness, causing more sugar cravings. It also makes some women less sensitive to salt, causing cravings for salty foods. Understanding this connection behind your cravings for salt and sugar may help you to not overindulge in them.

Symptom Soother: Tender Breasts

Sore and swollen breasts are often the first signs that you're pregnant. If you're uncomfortable, try an adjustable maternity bra as your breasts change and grow. Consider wearing a sports bra at night or using an extra pillow for comfort while sleeping. As your breasts can double in size during pregnancy, you'll probably need to increase your bra size, and switch to an encapsulation style sports bra (instead of compression style) if you don't wear one already.

How Much Weight to Gain

There's no one-weight-fits-all rule. The total amount of weight you should gain through your pregnancy depends on your pre-pregnancy weight. These recommendations are based on your pre-pregnancy body mass index (BMI).

IF YOU ARE . . .	WITH A BMI* OF . . .	YOU SHOULD GAIN
Underweight	< 18.5	28–40 lbs
Normal weight	18.5–24.9	25–35 lbs
Overweight	25–29.9	15–25 lbs
Obese	> 30	12–15 lbs
Carrying twins		35-45 lbs

*BMI = weight divided by (height in inches x height in inches) x 703

Baby Milestones

This week your embryo transitions to a stage of rapid growth and is now considered a fetus, albeit a teeny one. The intense developmental period of your baby's heart begins to slow, as the growth of other organs, bones, and muscles accelerates. Your baby's brain is now capable of involuntarily moving immature muscles (causing reflexive movements).

Stress Relief Tip If you're worrying about your baby's health and your pregnancy in general, get some exercise. Anxiety can raise levels of stress hormones that may harm the pregnancy, but exercise can help counter the effects. To reap the stress-reducing benefits, you need to work up a sweat and exercise at a level that causes mild breathlessness—you should be breathing heavy, but not huffing and puffing.

40

Keeping Fit Aim for five 30- to 45-minute sessions a week.

ACTIVITY	MONDAY	TUESDAY	WEDNESDAY	THURSDAY	FRIDAY	SATURDAY	SUNDAY
walking/ aerobic exercise							
yoga/ stretching							
strength training							

What is your sex life like now, and how has it
changed since you've been pregnant?

_____

_____

_____

_____

_____

_____

Has your morning sickness or any other symptoms interfered with your libido?

_____

_____

_____

_____

_____

_____

_____

_____

_____

_____

_____

week

11

Pregnancy Pointer

Coping with fatigue and morning sickness can be a real challenge, especially if you're working. Ask your partner to help out—getting him involved now will also make it easier to ask for help once your baby is born. He can do some of the cooking if he doesn't already, take over some of your household chores, and even exercise with you when you're feeling unmotivated.

Symptom Soother: Constipation

Rising progesterone slows down your digestion, potentially causing constipation—one of the most common symptoms of pregnancy. To help prevent and treat it, increase fiber in your diet (refer to week 7 for ideas) and when needed, take a fiber-based laxative such as Metamucil.

Stress Relief Tip

Start to collect names and contact information of women that you meet with a similar due date. You may find that you can help each other while pregnant, and develop friendships that continue after your delivery. These women may be especially important during the first few postpartum months.

Reminder
☐ Morning Sickness Questionnaire: page 197. Take twice this week.

Baby Milestones

Your baby's spine is beginning to straighten from a curved C into an upright position and his head is about half the length of his body. His eyelids are now formed and will soon fuse shut until your seventh month of pregnancy. His organs are rapidly developing and nerves are forming connections to muscles, which are beginning to move in a more coordinated fashion. Over the next nine weeks he will triple in length and increase his weight nearly thirty times.

Keeping Fit Aim for five 30- to 45-minute sessions a week.

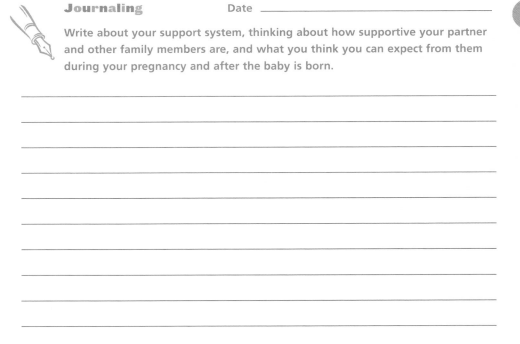

ACTIVITY	MONDAY	TUESDAY	WEDNESDAY	THURSDAY	FRIDAY	SATURDAY	SUNDAY
walking/ aerobic exercise							
yoga/ stretching							
strength training							

Journaling   Date _____

Write about your support system, thinking about how supportive your partner and other family members are, and what you think you can expect from them during your pregnancy and after the baby is born.

_____

_____

_____

_____

_____

_____

_____

_____

_____

_____

week 12

Pregnancy Pointer
A 15- to 30-minute walk after dinner will lower your insulin levels by as much as 50 percent and help prevent excessive weight gain and the development of insulin resistance—when your body has trouble moving sugar from your blood stream into your liver and muscles, where it's used or stored as energy. Insulin resistance can lead to gestational diabetes, large babies, and other complications. The evening constitutional will also help lower stress hormone levels.

! **Important** Cosmetics, nail polish, and other personal care products may contain chemicals that can enter your bloodstream and affect fetal development. Limit your exposure and use nail polish only in a well-ventilated area.

Stress Relief Tip You might not feel like the glowing mom-to-be now, but by your second trimester your energy and high spirits should return. This is a good time to plan a "babymoon," a before-baby getaway. Once your baby arrives you might not have the time or energy for a vacation for quite a while.

Reminder

☐ **Sleep Questionnaire:** If you're feeling tired, take the Pregnancy Sleep Risk Assessment on page 196 to make sure you're not sleep-deprived.

☐ **Morning Sickness Questionnaire:** Your nausea may have faded by now. If not, complete the morning sickness questionnaire on page 197. Have you seen an improvement?

Baby Milestones

The testes of a baby boy are now producing the male hormone, testosterone, and the ovaries of a baby girl are producing eggs. Your baby is only about the size of a strawberry. This week she will start moving amniotic fluid in and out of her lungs, practice for breathing, and she'll occasionally swallow it to stimulate her stomach and kidneys.

Keeping Fit Aim for five 30- to 45-minute sessions a week.

ACTIVITY	MONDAY	TUESDAY	WEDNESDAY	THURSDAY	FRIDAY	SATURDAY	SUNDAY
walking/ aerobic exercise							
yoga/ stretching							
strength training							

Journaling   Date _____

Write a letter to your unborn child, describing how you have felt during this trimester (you may decide never to show this to your child so be honest).

_____

_____

_____

_____

_____

_____

_____

46

week
13

Pregnancy Pointer

Some women become so afraid of gaining weight that they don't eat enough or they overexercise to compensate for their larger appetites. If you aggressively avoid weight gain by unhealthy calorie restriction at this phase of your pregnancy, you run the risk of delivering a child with intrauterine growth restriction (a small baby) and delayed neurological development. It will also increase your risk of preterm labor. If you're concerned that you've gained too much or aren't gaining enough or may have an eating disorder, ask your doctor for a referral to a dietician to analyze your needs.

Symptom Soother: Congestion

As your progesterone and estrogen levels climb, the membranes lining your nose will start to swell, causing congestion. Drink plenty of fluids to keep your nasal passages moist. For relief use a humidifier at night and saline nasal drops throughout the day.

Nutrition Questionnaire

Take the nutrition questionnaire on page 200 to evaluate your first trimester eating habits and see what areas may need improvement.

Reminder

☐ Mood Questionnaire: Page 198. See how your score compares to your previous score from week 9. Seek help if your scores are rising and your symptoms are getting worse.

Baby Milestones

Your baby's neck is getting longer and his head is now erect. He has formed baby teeth still hidden in his gums, and has developed vocal cords and taste buds. His legs are as long as his arms and all major body parts are forming.

Important Expectant women are susceptible to an infection from Listeria, a bacteria that can contaminate foods such as soft cheeses (Brie and Camembert, blue-veined cheeses, and Mexican style queso blanco fresco) and deli meats (hot dogs or smoked fish). Eat pasteurized cheese and foods heated to steam-producing temperatures to avoid this potentially serious infection.

Keeping Fit Aim for five 30- to 45-minute sessions a week.

ACTIVITY	MONDAY	TUESDAY	WEDNESDAY	THURSDAY	FRIDAY	SATURDAY	SUNDAY
walking/ aerobic exercise							
yoga/ stretching							
strength training							

49

Journaling   Date _____

Describe how you're feeling . . . have morning sickness and fatigue begun to lift?

_____

_____

_____

_____

_____

_____

_____

_____

_____

_____

_____

What was it like to hear your baby's heartbeat for the first time?

_____

_____

_____

_____

_____

_____

_____

What are your thoughts as you complete the first trimester?

_____

_____

_____

_____

_____

_____

_____

Third Prenatal Visit

THIS CAN BE AN EXCITING VISIT. You might hear your baby's heartbeat for the first time with a handheld Doppler pressed against your abdomen, and your practitioner can now feel the top of your growing uterus. She will also measure the height of your uterus (the fundal height), which rises as you approach your due date.

Here are some suggested questions to ask your practitioner:

Is my pregnancy proceeding normally?

Is my pregnancy considered "high risk"?

How much can I expect the fundal height to change every month?

Notes for this Prenatal Visit   Date _____

SYMPTOMS Write down any symptoms you have to discuss with your doctor, and then describe her response.

Symptoms

MD's response

51

Screening Tests

Your physician may talk to you about second trimester screening for birth defects or genetic disorders—these may be performed in addition to your first trimester screening.

THE QUAD PROFILE. Performed around the sixteenth to eighteenth week of pregnancy, the Quad Profile measures blood levels of four hormones—alpha-fetoprotein, estriol, HCG, and inhibin A. An abnormal result does not mean an abnormal pregnancy, but it will indicate if further testing, such as an amniocentesis or ultrasound, is warranted. If you're a vegetarian, have it noted on your lab slip as it can effect the interpretation of this test.

AMNIOCENTESIS. Between weeks 15 and 20, you may be advised to have an amniocentesis, in which a small amount of amniotic fluid is withdrawn through a long thin needle. An amniocentesis comes with a small risk of miscarriage—about one in every 200 to 400 procedures. Based upon the results, an ultrasound may still be recommended. (See page 66 for an alternative to the amnio.)

YOUR RESULTS

Your weight _____

Blood pressure _____

Urine test for sugar _____

Urine test for protein _____

Hemoglobin/hematocrit _____

Fetal heart rate _____

Fundal height _____

Notes After This Visit

Describe your thoughts about your visit or any important points your doctor made:

_____

_____

_____

_____

weeks **14** *to* **28**

THE MIDDLE THIRD OF YOUR pregnancy heralds the return of your vitality. You may feel even more energetic and have better spirits than you did before becoming pregnant. Symptoms of all kinds tend to diminish because the hormone shifts become subtler, and your belly hasn't expanded enough to start to feel uncomfortable. If you were waiting to make it through the first trimester to tell your friends you're pregnant, this can be a wonderful time of sharing and excitement, a chance to embrace your pregnancy. It's also, though, the time for prenatal screening for any birth defects, and this may bring a short spell of nervousness while you're awaiting your results.

>

weeks **14** *to* **28**

Your baby's organs are maturing and some are beginning to function. His body parts are forming—eyes,
ears, arms and legs—and by the end of this trimester,
he'll be fully formed—just in miniature. Now your baby
needs energy and nutrients to promote healthy growth
and brain development. And if you minimize the
unhealthy influences, you can help your baby develop
into a healthy, balanced person.

week 14

Pregnancy Pointer

If you're practicing high-intensity types of yoga, switch to a less strenuous prenatal yoga class like Hatha yoga, which will strengthen your core muscle groups using supported poses that are safe during pregnancy.

Healthy Eating for Two

Now that your baby is beginning to grow, you should start eating more calories. Take in 350 calories more than you did prepregnancy. This may sound like a lot, but it's not a license to eat whatever and whenever you feel the urge. Three hundred fifty calories is only the equivalent of:

1 banana with 2 tablespoons of peanut butter

1 modest slice of plain cheese pizza

½ cup vanilla frozen yogurt, topped with 1 tablespoon chocolate sauce.

53

Symptom Soother: Stretch Marks

Arising on your expanding belly and breasts, stretch marks are perhaps the most dreaded skin-deep drawback of pregnancy. You may be genetically predisposed to getting these squiggly and sometimes itchy lines, but you can take steps to prevent or minimize their appearance. Avoiding rapid and excessive weight gain can reduce their incidence or severity by 50 to 80 percent. Creams or lotions that contain *centella asiatica, panthenol,* or *menthol* may help reduce the number of stretch marks you get, and can also soothe the accompanying itch. Start rubbing the cream on your belly and breasts at the beginning of your second trimester.

Stress Relief Tip Now that you're through your first trimester, your risk of miscarriage is extremely low. You are well on your way to a healthy pregnancy, so if you were harboring any fears, now is the time to let them go and embrace your pregnancy.

Baby Milestones

Your baby's basic brain structure is complete, but her brain is not fully functional. Her hands are beginning to move voluntarily and smoothly, muscles in the cheek are forming, and the salivary glands are beginning to function. Her kidneys are beginning to produce urine and excrete it into the amniotic fluid, which replenishes itself every three hours

Keeping Fit Aim for five 30- to 45-minute sessions a week.

ACTIVITY	MONDAY	TUESDAY	WEDNESDAY	THURSDAY	FRIDAY	SATURDAY	SUNDAY
walking/ aerobic exercise							
yoga/ stretching							
strength training							

Journaling   Date _____

Freewrite on how it feels to put any concerns of miscarriage behind you and begin to enjoy being pregnant, or any new feelings you have about embracing your developing child.

_____

_____

_____

_____

_____

week

15

Pregnancy Pointer

As your belly expands, you are more susceptible to back pain. You can help prevent an achy back by trying not to gain excess weight and by exercising throughout your pregnancy—these two steps alone can cut your risk of low back pain by more than half. Eating less animal based food dramatically reduces the pain-inducing inflammatory chemicals in your blood, minimizing aches and pains.

Healthy Eating for Two

Omega-3 fatty acids help build nerve and brain cells. Docosahexaenoic acid (DHA), an important omega-3 for babies, makes up at least 40 percent of your baby's brain and about 60 percent of its optic nerves.

You'll need 300 mg DHA per day while pregnant (the omega-3 will also lower inflammatory chemicals that contribute to aches and pains). Since fish can contain high levels of toxins (see week 9), add flaxseed to your food and use a supplement like Expecta LIPIL.

Baby Milestones

Neurons are forming connections with one another in the developing brain at the rate of two million per second. Muscles and nerves are just beginning to communicate with one another, creating reflexes such as sucking, swallowing, and blinking. Cartilage—the early stages of bone—start to form, and will harden into bone gradually throughout the pregnancy and after delivery. If you are having a boy, his penis may now be recognizable during an ultrasound.

Important Don't forget to avoid secondhand smoke—studies have confirmed that it's just as harmful to your baby as if you were smoking yourself.

Symptom Soother:
Gum Disease Rising
progesterone levels can
make your gums tender and swollen.
Good oral hygiene can reduce the
risks of gum disease.

Be sure to:
Brush twice a day with a soft-bristled
brush and a fluoride toothpaste.

Floss or use an inter-dental device
daily.

Keeping Fit Aim for five 30- to 45-minute sessions a week.

ACTIVITY	MONDAY	TUESDAY	WEDNESDAY	THURSDAY	FRIDAY	SATURDAY	SUNDAY
walking/ aerobic exercise							
yoga/ stretching							
strength training							

57

Journaling   Date _____

Write about your thoughts on prenatal testing and any worries you are having
while waiting for results.

_____

_____

_____

_____

_____

_____

week 16

Pregnancy Pointer

Include strength training into your exercise program to make you stronger overall, and better able to push during childbirth. Use just enough weight or resistance so that you can complete two sets of 12 to 15 repetitions without straining. As you gain strength, add more repetitions or a third set. Avoid exercises that put stress on your abdominal muscles (like sit-ups) because the risk of muscle separation increases as your tummy gets bigger and the hormone relaxin makes your supportive ligaments more stretchy.

Healthy Eating for Two

High blood pressure during pregnancy can stress the blood vessels in the placenta as your pregnancy progresses. (The blood flow to your uterus increases from about half a gallon per hour to over 12 gallons per hour by your due date, putting more stress on your blood vessels). High blood pressure may lead to preeclampsia, a potentially life-threatening complication of pregnancy. By increasing your intake of the antioxidants, vitamins C and E, you can reduce your risk of preeclampsia by as much as 50 percent. Eat extra citrus fruits and for a boost of vitamin E, eat a small handful of almonds, hazelnuts, or peanuts every day.

Symptom Soother: Heartburn

As progesterone slows your digestion, you can get heartburn, that burning sensation in your chest. Progesterone also relaxes the valve at the top of your stomach, contributing to acid reflux. To minimize heartburn, eat small meals, drink most of your fluids between meals, avoid late-night snacks, and sleep with your head propped on pillows. Avoid foods like coffee and peppermint, which may worsen heartburn.

Baby Milestones
Your baby's back is nearly straight by now, though his legs remain curled up knees to chest in the fetal position. The bones of his neck continue to harden, supporting his head in an upright position. As his nerve-muscle connections become more sophisticated, his movement becomes voluntary and deliberate rather than random and uncontrolled.

Keeping Fit Aim for five 30- to 45-minute sessions a week.

ACTIVITY	MONDAY	TUESDAY	WEDNESDAY	THURSDAY	FRIDAY	SATURDAY	SUNDAY
walking/ aerobic exercise							
yoga/ stretching							
strength training							

Journaling   Date _____

How do you feel about your changing body?

_____

_____

_____

_____

_____

Are you looking forward to (or dreading) maternity clothes?

Do you have any concerns about your weight, how much—or little—you're gaining?

61

week 17

Pregnancy Pointer

Now's the time to start Kegel exercises, which strengthen your pelvic muscles for delivery and help prevent urinary incontinence. To get started, contract the muscles of your pelvis that you would use to stop urinating. Hold for 5 to 10 seconds. Do three to five sets of 5 to 10 contractions every day. An added benefit: Kegels may enhance your ability to have an orgasm.

Healthy Eating for Two

As your appetite returns with a vengeance, it's easy to overeat. Use these tips to avoid gaining too much weight: Eat slowly even if you feel ravenous; your brain takes 20 to 30 minutes to release the hormones that trigger satiation. Take smaller portions (during pregnancy, your eyes may be bigger than your stomach). Drink plenty of low calorie fluids; the brain often misinterprets dehydration as hunger since most natural foods contain a lot of water.

Symptom Soother: Bloating

If you are feeling bloated, you're probably not drinking enough water. Double your water intake for a day to flush the excess salt from your body.

Reminder

☐ Mood Questionnaire: Take the mood questionnaire on page 198 and see how it compares to your previous scores.

Baby Milestones

Your baby is now a bundle of energy, moving up to 50 times per hour while awake, and exploring his body and surroundings. He is about the size of your palm. His heart is beating 120 to 160 beats per minute, varying minute-by-minute, and circulating nearly 25 quarts of blood per day.

Keeping Fit Aim for five 30- to 45-minute sessions a week.

ACTIVITY	MONDAY	TUESDAY	WEDNESDAY	THURSDAY	FRIDAY	SATURDAY	SUNDAY
walking/ aerobic exercise							
yoga/ stretching							
strength training							

Journaling Date _____

Journal about your preferences for having a boy or girl,
and your thoughts on finding out the sex of your baby before delivery.

_____

_____

_____

_____

_____

_____

_____

_____

_____

_____

_____

IF YOU'RE HAVING second trimester screening, you might discuss the tests during this visit. If you have already had the tests and there are no complications, you'll have many weeks of smooth sailing ahead. Your baby's heartbeat should be easily detected this week, just above your pubic bone.

Here are some suggested questions to ask your practitioner:

Where do you recommend I go for prenatal classes?

Do you plan to perform an ultrasound to confirm my due dates?

Would you be willing to write me a prescription to rent a fetal Doppler for use at home?

How do you feel about 3D or 4D ultrasounds for keepsakes?

What medications are safe to take if I get a cold or cough?

Notes for this **Prenatal Visit**   Date _____

SYMPTOMS Write down any symptoms you have to discuss with your doctor, and then describe her response.

Symptoms   MD's response

_____   _____

_____   _____

_____   _____

_____   _____

_____   _____

_____   _____

_____   _____

Screening Tests

Some physicians recommend a genetic sonogram around weeks 18 to 20. This screening involves a comprehensive ultrasound that measures everything about your baby, and is usually performed at a special testing center. **By combining the ultrasound results with the quad screen, you can reduce the need for amniocentesis by nearly 70 percent.**

YOUR RESULTS

The following tests should be part of your second trimester care.

Your weight _____

Blood pressure _____

Urine test for sugar _____

Urine test for protein _____

Hemoglobin/hematocrit _____

Fetal heart rate _____

Fundal height _____

Notes After This Visit

Describe your thoughts about your visit or any important points your doctor made:

_____

_____

_____

_____

_____

_____

_____

_____

week 18

Pregnancy Pointer

The hormone *relaxin* will increase ten times during your pregnancy, peaking at about your thirty-sixth week. This hormone relaxes the joints of your pelvis to ease delivery, but it also loosens other joints—some by over 50 percent—potentially causing joint instability and injury. Switch to low-impact aerobics in order to minimize the stress on your joints. Avoid contact sports or activities that require sudden changes in direction or jarring motions. Remember to keep to a "conversational" pace and drink plenty of fluids.

Symptom Soother: Achy Joints

To reduce pain and inflammation around joints, eat more olive oil. Extra virgin olive oil (made from the first pressing), contains an anti-inflammatory chemical called *oleocanthal*, which has a similar, albeit milder, action as the anti-inflammatory drug ibuprofen. Try dipping bread in olive oil or drizzling it on your salad instead of a processed dressing.

Stress Relief Tip

Sex is a great way to relieve stress, but not if you're worried about hurting your baby. Rest assured, your baby is safely cushioned, but let comfort be your guide. Find positions that avoid your partner putting his weight on you or compressing your baby—these will also alleviate any discomfort with sex.

Baby Milestones

The nerves are becoming insulated so messages can be relayed faster along a greater distance without interruption as your baby grows. Your baby can now suck her thumb. Her fingertips have a unique set of *whorls* or fingerprints.

Keeping Fit Aim for five 30- to 45-minute sessions a week.

ACTIVITY	MONDAY	TUESDAY	WEDNESDAY	THURSDAY	FRIDAY	SATURDAY	SUNDAY
walking/ aerobic exercise							
yoga/ stretching							
strength training							

Journaling   Date _____

What do you and your husband do for fun now (you might want to look back at your life before children)?

_____

_____

_____

_____

_____

_____

_____

_____

_____

_____

_____

_____

How often do you go out for dinner, movies, do sports, or go to the gym?

_____

_____

_____

_____

_____

_____

_____

_____

_____

What are your current favorite movies, music, or books?

_____

_____

_____

_____

_____

_____

_____

_____

_____

_____

week 19

Pregnancy Pointer

Watch your balance when exercising; your growing baby will cause a shift in your center of gravity—increasing your risk of falling. Also avoid lying on your back when exercising since the weight of your uterus can compromise blood flow to your baby and reduce the return of blood flow to your heart.

Healthy Eating for Two Your baby is developing a greater need for amino acids, the building blocks of protein, to build his body. The protein you eat is broken down into these essential amino acids so they can easily cross the placenta. If your diet is low in protein, your body dips into your own protein stores—your muscles—to supply your baby with the necessary amino acids. Prevent muscle weakness by eating well.

Top protein boosters

1. Use seitan (wheat gluten) in place of beef or chicken in stir-fry.

2. Have organic peanut butter on a slice of toast.

3. Keep hard-boiled eggs in your refrigerator for a quick snack.

4. Sprinkle slivered toasted almonds over cereal or rice.

5. Add lentils to rice or couscous.

6. Whip up a smoothie using low-fat vanilla yogurt and frozen berries.

7. Drink hot cocoa made with nonfat milk.

8. Add beans or peas to soup.

Stress Relief Tip Schedule an afternoon at the spa. Let the spa staff know you are pregnant so they can give you the mom-to-be treatment you deserve (avoid hot tubs warmer than 103°F or saunas though).

 **Symptom Soother: Poor Sleep** As your pregnancy progresses, sleep becomes more difficult. If you have insomnia, try to reset your body clock by waking at the same time each morning. If you can't fall asleep, get up after 15 to 30 minutes rather than tossing and turning in bed, then return when you feel tired. A warm glass of milk at bedtime might help. Use a body-length pillow and sleep with a sports bra if your breasts need support. Try to sleep on your left side for maximal blood flow to the placenta.

Baby Milestones Heat-producing fat is beginning to be deposited under the skin of your baby's chest and neck to help regulate his body temperature. To protect his skin from the watery environment, soft, downy lanugo hairs will begin to cover his entire body. Hair will soon be visible in a distinct pattern on his scalp and eyebrows as well.

Keeping Fit Aim for five 30- to 45-minute sessions a week.

ACTIVITY	MONDAY	TUESDAY	WEDNESDAY	THURSDAY	FRIDAY	SATURDAY	SUNDAY
walking/ aerobic exercise							
yoga/ stretching							
strength training							

Journaling

Freewrite about whatever comes to mind.

week 20

Pregnancy Pointer As your abdomen advances, your back bears the brunt of the load. Weight gain can tug on your spine as the pliable joints in your pelvis shift to accommodate your belly. The result: an achy back. Good posture is important. Keep your shoulders pulled back and the pelvis tipped under you. Wear low-heeled shoes. When lifting objects from the floor or the trunk of your car, bend at your knees and hips and keep your back straight. Continue your fitness program, and if your back hurts, talk to your healthcare provider about specific exercises to strengthen your back muscles.

Stress Relief Tip Throughout your pregnancy, you might be frightened by what you read in the news or on the Internet—about dangers and risks during pregnancy, or you may get an earful from friends or family (women love to share their close-call childbirth stories). Before you panic, check the source, call your doctor, and discuss your concern. More often than not, any potential risk is very small or may not relate to your pregnancy.

! **Important** If you suffer from asthma, it is important to prevent attacks during pregnancy. The risk of attacks worsens between your sixth and eighth month of pregnancy. Talk to your provider about the best way to manage your symptoms so that your developing baby gets all the oxygen he needs. And don't stop using inhalers if you need them.

Baby Milestones
Your baby is forming sleep and wake patterns, and has discovered a favorite sleep position. If you're carrying a girl, her uterus is now fully formed and her ovaries have about 6 million eggs, the most she will have in her life. She weighs a little over 10 ounces and is 5½ to 6½ inches long crown-to-rump. Your uterus is growing and rising toward your belly button to accommodate her.

Keeping Fit Aim for five 30- to 45-minute sessions a week.

ACTIVITY	MONDAY	TUESDAY	WEDNESDAY	THURSDAY	FRIDAY	SATURDAY	SUNDAY
walking/ aerobic exercise							
yoga/ stretching							
strength training							

Journaling Date _____

Write about the sensation when you first felt the baby move. Where were you? Where in your belly did you feel it? Was it what you expected? If you haven't felt anything yet, you should in a couple of days. Come back to this page as soon as you do.

_____

_____

_____

_____

_____

_____

_____

_____

_____

_____

week

21

Pregnancy Pointer
If you've always been cold when your partner is warm, pregnancy will bring a cease-fire to the temperature wars. Rising progesterone raises your body heat throughout pregnancy, so you'll feel just as warm, if not warmer, than he does.

Healthy Eating for Two
Your developing baby can taste the flavors of your food through the amniotic fluid. By exposing him to a variety of healthy foods now, you may expand his newborn—and childhood—palate.

Reminder
☐ Mood Questionnaire: Take the mood questionnaire on page 198 and see how it compares to your previous scores. Seek help if your scores are rising and your symptoms are getting worse.

Symptom Soother: Bad Taste in Your Mouth Your heightened sense of taste and smell brought on by high levels of estrogen may also cause a bad or metallic taste in your mouth, called *dysguesia*. Keep crackers or gum in your purse to get rid of the taste. Be forewarned: Different foods might cause dysguesia as your tolerance changes.

Important As the urge to nest sets in, take a few precautions when decorating the nursery to avoid exposure to toxins. Avoid vintage painted furniture, which may contain lead. Try to recruit someone to paint for you but if you must do it yourself be sure to open the windows and keep the room well ventilated. No VOC (volatile organic compound) paint is the least toxic choice.

Baby Milestones
Your baby starts to absorb tiny amounts of nutrients in the amniotic fluid he swallows, although the umbilical cord remains his primary source of nutrients. His bone marrow now produces blood cells, and his legs are formed and will now grow in proportion to his body. His brain growth now takes off at an accelerated rate—a growth spurt that lasts until about five years after he's born.

Keeping Fit Aim for five 30- to 45-minute sessions a week.

ACTIVITY	MONDAY	TUESDAY	WEDNESDAY	THURSDAY	FRIDAY	SATURDAY	SUNDAY
walking/ aerobic exercise							
yoga/ stretching							
strength training							

Journaling   Date _____

What has been the most dramatic change in your life since you've become pregnant?

_____

_____

_____

_____

_____

_____

_____

_____

_____

_____

_____

_____

_____

If this is your second (or third) pregnancy, how does it compare to the first?

_____

_____

_____

_____

_____

_____

_____

Are there any food or drinks you're craving but not allowing yourself to indulge in?

_____

_____

_____

_____

_____

_____

_____

EVERYTHING SHOULD BE status quo during this visit. Your doctor may recommend an ultrasound that checks your baby's anatomy—the size, growth patterns, gender, and level of amniotic fluid. It's absolutely awesome because you can see your fully formed baby—and go home with an ultrasound to hang on your fridge. Your doctor will likely recommend a *glucose screening test* for gestational diabetes between the twenty-fourth and twenty-eighth week. This blood test measures your glucose level one hour after you drink a sugar solution (see week 24 for a yummy alternative).

Here are some suggested questions to ask your practitioner:

Is my pregnancy proceeding normally?

What types of symptoms should I call you about?

Is it okay to continue exercising?

Are there any problems that I'm at high risk of experiencing?

Notes for this **Prenatal Visit**   Date _____

SYMPTOMS Write down any symptoms you have to discuss with your doctor, and then describe her response.

Symptoms

MD's response

_____   _____

_____   _____

_____   _____

_____   _____

_____   _____

_____   _____

_____   _____

_____   _____

_____   _____

YOUR RESULTS

Your weight _____

Blood pressure _____

Urine test for sugar _____

Urine test for protein _____

Hemoglobin/hematocrit _____

Fetal heart rate _____

Fundal height _____

Notes After This Visit

Describe your thoughts about your visit or any important
points your doctor made:

_____

_____

_____

_____

_____

_____

_____

_____

_____

_____

_____

_____

_____

week 22

Healthy Eating for Two Think color when choosing fruits and veggies. Whole foods that are rich with deep color, like blueberries, pomegranates, and raspberries, contain healthy antioxidants—which can reduce the risk of preeclampsia.

Pregnancy Pointer Here are some of the benefits of continuing to exercise—in case you needed motivation.

- Lower risk of gestational diabetes and high blood pressure
- Faster recovery after delivery
- Improved digestion, less constipation
- Lower risk of depression
- Larger, healthier placenta and improved flow of nutrients to your baby
- Enhanced body image

Baby Milestones Your baby's brain and nerve endings are able to process the sensation of touch so she will stroke and grasp at anything in reach. She is approaching one pound and now has bright pink, wrinkly, parchmentlike skin lined with blood vessels. If you are having a boy, primitive sperm are beginning to develop.

Stress Relief Tip To relieve any concerns you have about your hospital or birthing center, ask for a tour. It's reassuring to view the birthing rooms and ask questions about the delivery and the care your newborn will receive in the nursery.

Keeping Fit Aim for five 30- to 45-minute sessions a week.

ACTIVITY	MONDAY	TUESDAY	WEDNESDAY	THURSDAY	FRIDAY	SATURDAY	SUNDAY
walking/ aerobic exercise							
yoga/ stretching							
strength training							

Journaling   Date _____

Write about the baby names you and your partner
are considering. Will the baby be named after someone?

_____
_____
_____
_____
_____
_____
_____
_____
_____
_____
_____
_____
_____

week 23

Pregnancy Pointer Pregnancy hormones can change the shape of the lenses of your eyes and alter your vision. If you wear contact lenses, you might need to switch to glasses while expecting. Once you deliver your vision should return to your prepregnancy "normal," so you may not need a new prescription.

Healthy Eating for Two
Your cravings for ice cream and other sweet treats may be escalating. Here's how to indulge without causing hormone chaos. Eat sweets directly after a meal so the fiber and protein of the meal help slow absorption of the sugar, tempering a sugar and insulin spike. Save your treat for the evening, when the post-sugar lull may help you wind down for bed.

Stress Relief Tip Family playtime is a great way to interact with your baby. First do some light activity so your baby becomes awake and active. Then lie down on your left side, providing the maximal blood supply to your baby. Have your partner rest his hand on your tummy and feel the baby move. Encourage him to give a gentle poke in response to any kicks or movements. It's normal for your baby to respond to these activities—the stimulation boosts his brain development.

Baby Milestones
The bones of the inner ear have hardened, and your child can now detect sound vibrations. He can hear the internal conversation of your gurgles and heartbeat. Your baby begins to produce surfactant, which lubricates the tiny pockets in the lungs so they can inflate and he can practice breathing with amniotic fluid.

Keeping Fit Aim for five 30- to 45-minute sessions a week.

ACTIVITY	MONDAY	TUESDAY	WEDNESDAY	THURSDAY	FRIDAY	SATURDAY	SUNDAY
walking/ aerobic exercise							
yoga/ stretching							
strength training							

Journaling Date _____

Freewrite about anything that comes to mind.

_____

_____

_____

_____

_____

_____

_____

_____

_____

_____

_____

_____

_____

week 24

Pregnancy Pointer If you can't stomach the overly sweet orange drink used for the glucose screening test, ask your doctor if you can use jelly beans. Several studies have found that eating eighteen jelly beans had the equivalent sugar jolt as the drink. The test measures your response to the surge in sugar.

Healthy Eating for Two To keep up on your DHA requirements of 300 mg per day, eat about seven DHA-fortified eggs each week from now through the twenty-eighth week of pregnancy. During this period DHA can reduce your chance of preterm labor and help prevent excessive weight gain by keeping blood sugars stabilized. It may also reduce your risk of postpartum depression.

Baby Milestones Your baby weighs in at one and a half pounds and measures 11½ to 12 inches long, crown to heel. Now that her inner ear is fully developed, she has a sense of balance and up versus down. Sweat glands are forming in the skin and creases are forming on her palms and soles.

! Important Work Safety during Pregnancy You will probably be able to work throughout most of your pregnancy as long as you and your baby remain healthy and free of complications. But as your pregnancy progresses, you may need to make some modifications, particularly if your job is strenuous or dangerous. Heavy physical lifting, straining, or carrying, and even prolonged standing may be risky. You should also know if your job exposes you to hazardous substances. Discuss these issues with your employer and learn what you can do to minimize your risk.

Keeping Fit Aim for five 30- to 45-minute sessions a week.

ACTIVITY	MONDAY	TUESDAY	WEDNESDAY	THURSDAY	FRIDAY	SATURDAY	SUNDAY
walking/ aerobic exercise							
yoga/ stretching							
strength training							

Journaling Date _____

What is your sex life like now, and how has it changed since the first trimester?

_____
_____
_____
_____
_____
_____
_____
_____
_____
_____
_____
_____

Has your partner's body changed? (Some men gain weight when their partners are pregnant, a phenomenon known as Couvades syndrome.)

week

25

Pregnancy Pointer If you find it is difficult to set aside 30 minutes for exercise, break it up into two to three sessions of activity. The benefits to you and your baby are the same as if you worked out all at once.

Flexitarian Tip When you eat a plant-based diet, you get a lot more protein than you may realize. Take a look.

5 GREAT PLANT BASED PROTEIN SOURCES

	(% of calories coming from protein)
Spinach	49%
Broccoli	45%
Soybeans	35%
Mushrooms	34%
Green peas	28%

Baby Milestones
The supportive structures of the spine are beginning to form a protective barrier for the spinal cord. Loud noises will startle your baby; you might be able to feel him move in response to noise, like when you're at the movies or listening to loud music. His toenails and fingernails are growing in.

Stress Relief Tip Dreams during the second trimester often involve baby animals or love affairs, or they're very frightening. Try to write down any intense dreams you have during your second trimester. Also write down any associations to your feelings that come up.

Reminder

☐ Mood Questionnaire: page 198. See how your scores compare with previous weeks.

Keeping Fit Aim for five 30- to 45-minute sessions a week.

ACTIVITY	MONDAY	TUESDAY	WEDNESDAY	THURSDAY	FRIDAY	SATURDAY	SUNDAY
walking/ aerobic exercise							
yoga/ stretching							
strength training							

Journaling   Date _____

Write about your thoughts on being a stay-at-home mom versus returning to work after your maternity leave (your thoughts may change after your baby is born).

_____

_____

_____

_____

_____

_____

THIS VISIT IS OFTEN a great time to discuss nutrition and weight gain. If you are concerned you are gaining too much (or not enough) weight, your practitioner might refer you to a dietician. In addition, if your blood type is Rh-negative, you will receive a RhoGAM shot sometime between the twenty-eighth and twenty-ninth week to prevent complications. Ask your healthcare provider if you will need this injection.

Here are some suggested questions to ask your practitioner:

Am I gaining the appropriate amount of weight?

Do you recommend I see a dietician or make any changes in my diet?

How long can I continue my regular schedule and responsibilities at work?

Notes for this **Prenatal Visit**   Date _____

SYMPTOMS Write down any symptoms you have to discuss with your doctor, and then describe her response.

Symptoms   MD's response

_____   _____

_____   _____

_____   _____

_____   _____

_____   _____

_____   _____

_____   _____

_____   _____

YOUR RESULTS

Your weight _____

Blood pressure _____

Urine test for sugar _____

Urine test for protein _____

Fetal heart rate _____

Fundal height _____

Notes After This Visit

Describe your thoughts about your visit or any important
points your doctor made:

_____
_____
_____
_____
_____
_____
_____
_____
_____
_____
_____
_____
_____
_____

week
26

Pregnancy Pointer Pregnancy may put you at risk of sleep apnea, when your breathing stops momentarily as you sleep. Sleep apnea may be an indication of gestational diabetes, preeclampsia, or fetal growth restriction. If your partner reports that you're snoring or you have brief episodes in which you stop breathing, talk to your doctor.

Symptom Soother: Skin Changes You may have noticed some changes to your skin tone. Rising levels of melanocyte-stimulating hormone during pregnancy can darken pigmented skin, like the nipples and areola, genitals, moles, and freckles. You may also get *melasma,* also known as the "mask of pregnancy," because skin on your forehead, cheeks, and chin darken. Sun exposure can worsen melasma. And the *linea nigra,* a dark pigmented line from your navel to your pubic bone, often appears during the second trimester. Fortunately, most of these discolorations fade after delivery as hormone levels return to normal. However, if you notice any moles changing shape or size, notify your healthcare provider.

Risk for Preterm Labor Questionnaire

You may be at high risk of preterm labor. If you are, it's important to know as there are some preventive steps you can take. Take the questionnaire on page 202. If your results indicate that you may be at risk, talk to your healthcare provider to review your options.

Baby Milestones

The retina of your baby's eyes are fully developed, allowing her to respond to a light held up to your belly. Her eyelids will open in a week or two and the nostrils will soon open as well. She can "hear" the vibrations of deep sounds, like a man's voice, through your belly. She weighs 1.7 to 2 pounds and is approximately 14 inches long crown to heel.

Keeping Fit Aim for five 30- to 45-minute sessions a week.

ACTIVITY	MONDAY	TUESDAY	WEDNESDAY	THURSDAY	FRIDAY	SATURDAY	SUNDAY
walking/ aerobic exercise							
yoga/ stretching							
strength training							

Journaling　　　　　Date _____

Journal about your mother and how she will be a part of your pregnancy and your life with your new baby. If you have a poor relationship with her or she is deceased, write about those feelings.

95

_____

_____

_____

_____

_____

_____

_____

_____

_____

_____

_____

week 27

Pregnancy Pointer Travel safely. In a car, always wear a seat belt. The lap belt should rest beneath your belly, the shoulder strap between your breasts and to the side of your abdomen. Do not turn off the air bags but do move the seat back as far as possible from the steering wheel to accommodate your growing baby. For air travel, reserve an aisle seat and check if the airline has any restrictions on pregnant women. Don't plan to fly the last month of pregnancy in case you go into labor. Take water, a snack, and a pillow for comfort. Due to a higher risk of blood clots during pregnancy, stretch your legs or walk every 30 minutes to keep your blood moving.

Healthy Eating for Two Avoid hydrogenated fats, otherwise known as *trans fats,* a man-made fat prevalent in lard, shortening, margarine, and many fried foods and packaged cookies, crackers, and other baked goods. Trans fats are oils that have been given an extra hydrogen bond that keeps them solid. But they build up in your blood vessels—not only the ones to your heart and brain, but also the ones to your uterus—contributing to damaged or blocked arteries.

Baby Milestones Since the twelfth week of pregnancy, your baby has tripled or even quadrupled in size. The immune system will soon begin maturing to help protect against infections, but you've transferred enough protection through your own antibodies to help protect against illness for up to six months after birth.

Symptom Soother: Fatigue As your baby grows, you'll tend to take shallow breaths and not fully expand your lungs. This can raise the amount of carbon dioxide in your blood, making you feel lethargic. If you find you're getting sleepy, try taking ten deep breaths, fully expanding your rib cage. This should give you the oxygen oomph to keep going.

Keeping Fit Aim for five 30- to 45-minute sessions a week.

ACTIVITY	MONDAY	TUESDAY	WEDNESDAY	THURSDAY	FRIDAY	SATURDAY	SUNDAY
walking/ aerobic exercise							
yoga/ stretching							
strength training							

Journaling

Date _____

Write about the sensation when you feel your baby move now. How would you describe it? (Look back at week 20 and see how the sensation compares.)

_____

_____

_____

_____

_____

_____

_____

_____

_____

_____

_____

_____

_____

Have people tried to touch your belly, and how did that make you feel?

Have you received unwanted advice, and how did that make you feel?

Pregnancy Pointer You may have found that your eyes well up (if you're not outright bawling) at the movies—or in response to a heart-tugging commercial. During the second trimester, prolactin and oxytocin, hormones that are linked to bonding, begin to rise in preparation for breast-feeding. One side effect is a tendency for compassion and tearfulness.

Healthy Eating for Two If you have a sweet tooth, consider artificial sweeteners. Non-nutritive sweeteners add sweetness without the calories and without triggering insulin fluctuations (complete avoidance of sweets can lead to feeling deprived and then overeating). Splenda is an artificial sweetener that tastes about 600 times sweeter than sugar. It has been more thoroughly researched than other sweeteners and appears to be safe during pregnancy. It is not chemically broken down, absorbed, accumulated in your body, or transmitted through your breast milk.

Symptom Soother: Swollen Feet and Ankles Fluid pools in your feet, especially after standing for 30 minutes or more, because your uterus partly blocks blood returning to your heart, causing a backup in your feet. Water aerobics or simply standing in a pool can do wonders. Deep water applies pressure to your skin, coaxing the excess fluid back in to your blood vessels where it can be excreted into your urine. So don't be surprised if you have to use the restroom after a dip in the pool.

Important Your kidneys must work double time to flush away waste products (yours and your baby's). Add to that the growing pressure from your uterus and you'll find yourself running to the bathroom with annoying frequency. It might be tempting to cut back on how much you drink, but your body and your growing baby's body depends on you to stay hydrated.

Nutrition Questionnaire

Take the Nutrition Questionnaire on page 200 to evaluate your second trimester eating habits compared to the first trimester. How have you done and what areas do you need improvement?

Baby Milestones

Your baby's eyes are beginning to open and close and he is settling into a pattern of sleep and rest, dozing off for up to 30 minutes at a time. Your voice is now recognizable and he can respond to your sounds. He has little over 2 percent body fat and has reached most of his length.

Keeping Fit Aim for five 30- to 45-minute sessions a week.

ACTIVITY	MONDAY	TUESDAY	WEDNESDAY	THURSDAY	FRIDAY	SATURDAY	SUNDAY
walking/ aerobic exercise							
yoga/ stretching							
strength training							

Journaling   Date _____

Write a letter to your unborn child, describing how you have felt during this trimester and what you are thinking about.

_____

_____

THIS VISIT your healthcare provider may examine your skin for swelling or varicose veins. She will probably discuss weight gain and diet issues with you.

Here are some suggested questions to ask your practitioner:

Do you recommend I write a birth plan, and are you willing to work with it? How do you feel about doulas? Do you have one to recommend?

How can I tell if my contractions are Braxton Hicks "practice" contractions or true contractions of labor?

What modifications should I make to my exercise routine?

Notes for this **Prenatal Visit**   Date _____

SYMPTOMS Write down any symptoms you have to discuss with your doctor, and then describe her response.

Symptoms   MD's response

_____   _____

_____   _____

_____   _____

_____   _____

_____   _____

_____   _____

_____   _____

_____   _____

_____   _____

_____   _____

YOUR RESULTS

Your weight _____

Blood pressure _____

Urine test for sugar _____

Urine test for protein _____

Fetal heart rate _____

Fundal height _____

Notes After This Visit

Describe your thoughts about your visit or any important
points your doctor made:

_____

_____

_____

_____

_____

_____

_____

_____

_____

_____

_____

_____

_____

_____

AS YOU ENTER your third trimester, you'll likely begin to think about your labor and delivery. As you consider your options, you can create a birth plan; a list of your preferences for labor and delivery, as well as for the care for your baby while in the hospital. Having a birth plan will help guide you and your delivery team through your childbirth. It's especially helpful to turn to when you need to make quick decisions but are exhausted and are not thinking clearly. Start working on your birth plan now. Sit down with your partner and explore your labor and delivery options and preferences. Show this to your practitioner before your delivery so she can go over any potential issues and approve certain options (such as eating during labor). Be sure to look into the availability of these options where you plan to deliver; some facilities might prohibit certain procedures.

Delivery

1. Whom do you want to attend your labor and delivery?

2. Do you plan to hire a doula, a labor coach?

3. Are you planning a vaginal delivery, a VBAC (vaginal birth after cesarean), or scheduled cesarean section?

4. What are your preferences for holding your baby immediately after delivery versus having the baby cleaned and taken care of on a warming table?

105

Vaginal Delivery

1. How do you feel about using drugs to induce labor?

_____

_____

_____

2. What are your preferences for helping you through labor (music, walking, dim lights)?

_____

_____

_____

3. Do you want continuous or intermittent fetal monitoring?

_____

_____

4. What are your preferences for pain relief during labor? Be specific about when and under what conditions you want to take pain medication.

_____

_____

_____

5. How do you feel about an episiotomy, a surgical cut made to widen the opening of the birth canal?

_____

_____

6. Do you have any coaching or position preferences while you are pushing?

_____

_____

_____

Cesarean Delivery

1. Do you have a preferred method of anesthesia?

_____

_____

2. Do you have a preferred anesthesiologist?

_____

3. Do you want the baby brought to you in the recovery room, and how many minutes after the birth?

_____

Baby

1. Do you have any specific preferences for your baby's first hour after birth?

_____

_____

_____

2. Do you plan to breast-feed or bottle-feed?

_____

_____

3. Do you want the baby to be given a pacifier in the nursery?

_____

4. What are your preferences for nighttime feedings?

_____

_____

5. How do you feel about rooming in with your baby?

_____

_____

Journaling

Write about your hopes or concerns surrounding your childbirth. While social debate may simmer over the best way to have a baby (there are *many* points of view regarding the decision to use pain medication), try to put this aside and focus on what feels right to you. At the end of the day, all would agree that what is most important is having a healthy baby.

weeks **29** *to* **40**

(up to week 42)

THE THIRD TRIMESTER IS filled with mounting excitement as your due date approaches. The first month or so is a wonderful time for many women, who become more focused on the baby—as he's making his presence felt by his sheer size and more noticeable kicks and jabs to your belly. The reality of a fully developed baby who will soon be in your arms begins to set in. But as you progress through the trimester, your energy begins to fade as your belly expands farther than you thought was possible. Aches and pains can also arise as your weight pulls at your back and your joints loosen. And there's simply a lot to consider—creating a birth plan for your labor and delivery, decorating ❯

weeks **29** *to* **40**

(up to week 42)

the baby's room, and getting equipped with all the newborn essentials.

   As for the baby, his development is centered around growth and maturation of key organs, like his lungs. This is an important time for the development of his brain, and it's the time when he begins to store hormonal information—in a sense he's being pro-grammed with baseline norms for his metabolism. It's an important time to eat healthy, avoid excess weight gain, to exercise, and to minimize stress—so you are your healthiest and so your baby is developing in the healthiest environment possible.

week 29

Healthy Eating for Two During your final trimester your insulin levels will rise 200 to 300 percent higher than your prepregnancy levels in order to channel more sugar to your baby to support his growth. But if you are already overweight, this added insulin provides too much glucose to your baby, potentially contributing to obesity later in his life. The following tips will help improve your body's response to insulin and improve your baby's hormone balance.

EAT TWO TO THREE BRAZIL NUTS A DAY. They contain selenium, a mineral that improves the movement of glucose into cells. Brown rice and whole grains contain selenium as well. You need about 60 mcg each day.

DRESS YOUR SALAD. A tablespoon or two of vinegar each day enhances the breakdown of sugar for several hours, helping to lower insulin resistance.

GET CHROMIUM. This mineral helps insulin move glucose into cells where it is used as fuel. You can get the recommended 30 mcg per day by eating whole grains, brewer's yeast, wheat germ, and egg yolks.

AVOID HIGH FRUCTOSE CORN SYRUP. This super sweetener is found in many processed foods and causes huge spikes in your insulin levels.

Pregnancy Pointer Weight gain during this last trimester is primarily from your growing baby, who will double in size. Expect to gain about one half to one pound per week until your due date. Increase your calorie intake another 150 calories per day.

That's the equivalent of

6 walnuts
½ cup whole wheat pasta with
   ½ cup marinara sauce

½ cup brown rice with 1 cup
   mixed vegetables
Just under 1 ounce of dark chocolate

Important Severe headaches accompanied by blurry vision and considerable swelling of your feet, ankles, or hands could indicate the beginning of preeclampsia. Call your physician immediately if you have these symptoms.

Reminder

☐ Mood Questionnaire: page 198.

Baby Milestones

During the third trimester of brain development, the hypothalamus becomes active. This region controls many internal functions such as temperature regulation, hormone balance, and breathing.

Keeping Fit Aim for five 30- to 45-minute sessions a week.

ACTIVITY	MONDAY	TUESDAY	WEDNESDAY	THURSDAY	FRIDAY	SATURDAY	SUNDAY
walking/ aerobic exercise							
yoga/ stretching							
strength training							

110

Journaling　　　Date _____

What has been the most surprising change in your body?

_____

_____

_____

_____

_____

Has being pregnant changed how you feel about yourself as a woman?

What are surprising comments you hear from friends and family?
What about from strangers?

week

30

Pregnancy Pointer Preterm birth—defined as delivering before your thirty-seventh week—occurs in as many as 12 percent of all pregnancies. You can make several diet and lifestyle changes to reduce your own risk of preterm labor. Stick to a diet low in animal fat and high in grains. Keep well hydrated and continue taking your prenatal vitamin with folic acid. Low levels of folic acid in the third trimester are associated with preterm labor. Lastly, take steps to reduce your stress and spend time resting with your feet up to ease the pressure on your cervix.

Healthy Eating for Two
Your baby will be born with 300 bones (some will eventually fuse together resulting in 206). For cartilage to harden into bone, your baby needs calcium. Aim to get 1,300 mg of calcium a day so your body doesn't tap into your own bones for this key mineral. Excellent food sources of calcium include:

Food	Calcium (mg)
¾ cup whole grain Total cereal	1000
½ cup calcium-fortified tofu	861
1 cup milk	300
1 slice whole wheat bread	190

Symptom Soother: Gas As your digestion slows, you may experience more gas, which can make you feel bloated and uncomfortable. To ease your discomfort, drink warm peppermint tea, avoid high fat foods, eat small, frequent meals, and treat constipation by increasing fiber or taking a fiber supplement.

Baby Milestones
Your baby will start to swallow up to a quart of amniotic fluid per day, providing her developing digestive system with plenty of practice. The soft lanugo hair will begin to disappear from all but your baby's back and shoulders.

Stress Relief Tip Many women worry that having an orgasm increases the risk of preterm labor. Though some of the "feel-good" hormones released during orgasm can trigger uterine contractions, these contractions won't progress into labor unless you are at term. Progesterone keeps your uterine muscles relaxed enough to serve as a buffer against many of the causes of preterm labor.

Keeping Fit Aim for five 30- to 45-minute sessions a week.

ACTIVITY	MONDAY	TUESDAY	WEDNESDAY	THURSDAY	FRIDAY	SATURDAY	SUNDAY
walking/ aerobic exercise							
yoga/ stretching							
strength training							

Journaling   Date _____

Freewrite about whatever comes to mind.

_____

_____

_____

_____

_____

_____

YOUR VISITS WILL OCCUR once every two weeks now. During these visits, your practitioner may palpate your uterus to determine the position of your baby. Late in your pregnancy glucose imbalances can become serious if not identified. Talk to your healthcare provider to see if you need to repeat the glucose screening test during week 34.

Here are some suggested questions to ask your practitioner on either visit:

What is your protocol if I go beyond my due date?

When do you consider inducing labor?

What percentage of your patients have epidurals?

Do you routinely intervene in labor?

What are your thoughts on allowing foods or liquids during labor?

What position is my baby in?

115

Notes for the
Eighth Prenatal Visit

Date _____

SYMPTOMS Write down any symptoms you have to discuss with your doctor, and then describe her response.

Symptoms   MD's response

_____   _____

_____   _____

_____   _____

_____   _____

_____   _____

_____   _____

_____   _____

YOUR RESULTS

Your weight _____

Blood pressure _____

Urine test for sugar _____

Urine test for protein _____

Fetal heart rate _____

Fundal height _____

Notes for the
Ninth Prenatal Visit

Date _____

SYMPTOMS Write down any symptoms you have to discuss with your doctor,
and then describe her response.

Symptoms

MD's response

_____   _____

_____   _____

_____   _____

_____   _____

_____   _____

YOUR RESULTS

Your weight _____

Blood pressure _____

Urine test for sugar _____

Urine test for protein _____

Fetal heart rate _____

Fundal height _____

week 31

Pregnancy Pointer

It might seem early to be thinking about postpartum depression, but it's important to know if you are susceptible so you can prepare for it and take steps to reduce your risk. If you have any of these risk factors or are already showing signs of depression, talk to your doctor. Also try to keep stress under control, get plenty of sleep, and exercise.

Top 10 Risk Factors for Postpartum Depression

1. History of premenstrual syndrome

2. Depression during pregnancy

3. Low self-esteem

4. Stress associated with childcare

5. Anxiety during pregnancy

6. Life stress (occupational, social, or financial)

7. Limited support from friends and family

8. Marital stress

9. History of depression prior to pregnancy

10. Infant fussiness

 Flexitarian Tip To minimize your risk of preeclampsia, now's the time to reduce your fat intake. Fat is calorie dense (one teaspoon of oil, fat, or butter contains about 45 calories) and excess calories lead to the production of more free radicals, which have been found to damage the placenta and the blood vessels that serve it. This damage can reduce blood flow, leading to preeclampsia. Make sure that fat accounts for no more than 20 to 25 percent of your daily calorie intake. Cut back on unhealthy saturated fats by eating less animal fat and avoiding tropical oils (coconut, palm kernel, and palm), most often found in processed snack foods.

 Important Modify your exercise so that blood flow to your baby is not compromised. Avoid inverted yoga poses or other exercises in which you're lying flat on your back. Also reduce the amount of weight you are lifting to avoid straining your joints that are not more lax as you get closer to your due date.

Stress Relief Tip If you're feeling stressed out, try to fit prenatal yoga classes into your week. One 25- to 30-minute session can reduce stress hormones by up to 80 percent. Yoga also encourages slow deep breathing, which is helpful during the third trimester, when your breathing is more shallow—it also helps reduce anxiety.

Baby Milestones
This week begins a period of rapid brain growth. About 20 percent of the energy your baby consumes will fuel her brain. Nerve endings in her ears are now connected, allowing her to hear sounds rather than just feel the vibration of sounds.

Keeping Fit Aim for five 30- to 45-minute sessions a week.

ACTIVITY	MONDAY	TUESDAY	WEDNESDAY	THURSDAY	FRIDAY	SATURDAY	SUNDAY
walking/ aerobic exercise							
yoga/ stretching							
strength training							

Journaling   Date _____

Write about your feelings on pain relief during labor and delivery. Think about the various influences on your choices.

_____

_____

_____

week
32

Healthy Eating for Two Your baby requires about 1000 mg of iron for the normal growth and development of his brain. If your practitioner has recommended an iron supplement because you show signs of low iron, be sure to take it. You should also boost your diet with iron-fortified foods, green leafy vegetables, legumes, prunes, and blackstrap molasses (add some to baked beans or oatmeal).

Pregnancy Pointer Light to moderate exercise at least three times a week can feel challenging as your tummy grows, but try to keep it up. Exercise can benefit your labor and delivery in these ways:

- **One-third shorter labor**

- **35 percent reduced need for pain medications**

- **50 percent reduced need to induce labor**

- **Increased likelihood of full-term birth (versus preterm or post-due-date births)**

120

Aches and Pain Index Many healthcare providers delay treating back or pelvic pain until after delivery. Yet persistent pain can affect your quality of life and turn into a chronic problem that lasts long after childbirth. If you're experiencing any pain, take the Aches and Pain Index on page 203. Retake this once a week to see if your problem is improving, worsening, or staying the same. If your symptoms worsen, discuss your treatment options with your doctor.

Sleep Questionnaire Fatigue may begin to set in again. If you're feeling tired, take the Pregnancy Sleep Risk Assessment on page 196 to make sure you're not sleep deprived. If you are, it can make you more sensitive to your aches and pains.

Baby Milestones

Your baby's five senses—smell, taste, sight, touch, and hearing—are all functioning (though stimuli are perceived slightly differently in a liquid environment).

His body is storing the minerals, calcium, iron, and phosphorus to aid the healthy development of bones, teeth and muscles. Your baby's fingers and toes have nails and his scalp is filling in with hair.

Keeping Fit Aim for five 30- to 45-minute sessions a week.

ACTIVITY	MONDAY	TUESDAY	WEDNESDAY	THURSDAY	FRIDAY	SATURDAY	SUNDAY
walking/ aerobic exercise							
yoga/ stretching							
strength training							

Journaling

Date _____

Write about any apprehensions you have about labor and delivery. Describe the excitement you are feeling about the big event.

_____
_____
_____
_____
_____
_____

_____

_____

_____

_____

_____

_____

_____

_____

Whom do you want to be with you during your labor—your partner, a doula, your mom, and why?

_____

_____

_____

_____

_____

_____

_____

_____

_____

_____

_____

_____

_____

week 33

Pregnancy Pointer After your baby is born, your partner might experience some anxieties in his new role as dad and support person. Talk to him now about ways that he can enjoy his role as a father while also helping you get some much-needed rest. He can do one or two late-night feedings (a chance to bond with baby), chip in with burping the baby and changing her diaper after feedings during the day if he's taking time off from work, and he can help entertain guests, while you take your much-needed naps.

Kick Counting

Counting kicks is a simple at-home way to check in on your baby's movement and health. Do it whenever you are curious, concerned, or think you haven't felt a kick for a while. For added reassurance, do it twice a week. Refer to page 204 for instructions on how and when to count kicks.

123

Symptom Soother: Constipation

In your last trimester, constipation can make you feel very uncomfortable, and put you at risk for hemorrhoids, varicose veins of the rectum. Boost your intake of insoluble fiber, the kind that doesn't dissolve in water, to help move food through your system. Whole grain breakfast cereal, wheat bran, fruits, and vegetables are good choices. Make sure you drink plenty of fluids and try to exercise each day.

Baby Milestones

Your baby weighs nearly 4½ pounds. His skin color will soon be pink (a transition from dark red) and his wrinkles are starting to smooth out. By now the pupil of the eye constricts in response to light. When you talk, your baby is listening in and his heartbeat will increase in response.

Reminder

☐ Mood Questionnaire: page 198.

Keeping Fit Aim for five 30- to 45-minute sessions a week.

ACTIVITY	MONDAY	TUESDAY	WEDNESDAY	THURSDAY	FRIDAY	SATURDAY	SUNDAY
walking/ aerobic exercise							
yoga/ stretching							
strength training							

Journaling Date _____

Write about your thoughts on breast-feeding versus bottle-feeding, what it means for you to breast-feed, and how you might feel if you don't or can't.

_____

_____

_____

_____

_____

_____

_____

_____

_____

week 34

 Symptom Soother: An "Outie" Your "innie" belly button may now be an "outie" due to the rounding out of your belly. Rest assured, shortly after you deliver, your navel will return to its prepregnancy position. If the newly exposed skin is tender, consider covering it with a Band-Aid to prevent chafing.

Important Low levels of folic acid might make you susceptible to preterm labor. Keep taking your prenatal vitamins with folic acid.

126

Reminder
☐ Aches and Pain Index: page 203.
☐ Kick Counting: page 204.

Baby Milestones By now all major organs (except the lungs) are mature. Your baby has less room to move, so she will rest with her chin on her chest with arms crossed and legs drawn up toward her tummy and crossed. She can't tumble around with ease anymore but you should feel kicks every day. Your baby will soon orient her head to face down toward the birth canal in preparation for delivery.

Stress Relief Tip Dreams during the third trimester are easier to recall since you will be waking frequently from a kick to the ribs or to use the bathroom. Your dreams may involve large animals, driving oversized vehicles, or large or odd-shaped buildings. You may even dream of giving birth to a full-grown baby.

Keeping Fit Aim for five 30- to 45-minute sessions a weeky.

ACTIVITY	MONDAY	TUESDAY	WEDNESDAY	THURSDAY	FRIDAY	SATURDAY	SUNDAY
walking/ aerobic exercise							
yoga/ stretching							
strength training							

Journaling   Date _____

Freewrite on the following pages, writing whatever comes to mind.

_____

_____

_____

_____

_____

_____

_____

_____

_____

_____

_____

_____

_____

THE FREQUENCY of your prenatal visits will depend on how your pregnancy is progressing. It might be once every two weeks or once a week. Your practitioner may perform a pelvic exam to monitor the dilation (widening) and effacement (thinning) of your cervix.

Additional Tests

Your doctor will test you for group B streptococcus between your thirty-fifth and thirty-sixth week. This bacterium is harmless to adults but can pose a serious health threat if passed onto your newborn. The test involves a swab of your vagina or rectum; if you test positive you will be given antibiotics during your labor.

Notes for the Tenth Prenatal Visit

Date _____

SYMPTOMS Write down any symptoms you have to discuss with your doctor, and then describe her response.

Symptoms

MD's response

YOUR RESULTS

Your weight _____

Blood pressure _____

Urine test for sugar _____

Urine test for protein _____

Fetal heart rate _____

Fundal height _____

Pelvic exam _____

Notes for the
Eleventh Prenatal Visit

Date _____

SYMPTOMS Write down any symptoms you have to discuss with your doctor, and then describe her response.

Symptoms

MD's response

_____   _____

_____   _____

_____   _____

_____   _____

YOUR RESULTS

Your weight _____

Blood pressure _____

Urine test for sugar _____

Urine test for protein _____

Fetal heart rate _____

Fundal height _____

Pelvic exam _____

week 35

Pregnancy Pointer Your baby will soon move lower into your pelvis, a process called *lightening.* As her head drops, you may feel the urge to urinate more often (you may even leak some urine—don't forget your Kegels). The good news: Your lungs and diaphragm will have more room to expand, making breathing easier.

Stress Relief Tip Rising levels of *estriol,* a weak form of estrogen that's produced during pregnancy, along with rising levels of the milk-producing hormone prolactin, can dim the lights on your libido. Don't take it to heart—and let your partner know the culprit in your dampened libido. There are many ways to express your love such as snuggling, kissing, touching, or massage.

131

Baby Milestones
Your baby's lungs are almost completely developed. The fat deposits are filling out his skin. About 15 percent of his body weight is fat, which is necessary to maintain his stable body temperature. If you are having a boy, his testes will fully descend in the next few weeks.

Sympton Soother: Restless Leg Syndrome One in four women experience a jittery, tingling sensation in their legs (and occasionally in their arms) called restless leg syndrome (RLS). It causes an uncontrollable urge to move your legs. It worsens at rest or during the night and tends to peak late in the third trimester, robbing you of precious sleep time. If you have RLS, regular exercise and stretching exercises can help relieve it. Talk to your healthcare provider about taking an iron supplement, since a deficiency in this mineral is one possible cause of RLS.

Reminder

☐ Kick Counting: Refer to page 204 for instructions.

Keeping Fit Aim for five 30- to 45-minute sessions a week.

ACTIVITY	MONDAY	TUESDAY	WEDNESDAY	THURSDAY	FRIDAY	SATURDAY	SUNDAY
walking/ aerobic exercise							
yoga/ stretching							
strength training							

132

Journaling Date _____

What is your sex life like now, and how has it changed since the first trimester?

_____
_____
_____
_____
_____
_____
_____
_____
_____
_____

week 36

Healthy Eating for Two By now there is little room in your abdomen for your stomach to expand to accommodate a full meal. To get the necessary number of calories and nutrients, switch to five or six mini-meals a day. Grazing will also help curb heartburn and indigestion.

Sympton Soother: Fatigue Make an extra effort to drink water, especially when you feel like you're dragging. When you are pregnant, your kidneys produce three times as much of the diuretic hormone *aldosterone,* which increases urine production. This contributes to dehydration—a major cause of third trimester fatigue.

Reminder

☐ **Aches and Pain Index:** If you're experiencing pain, take the Aches and Pain Index on page 203.

☐ **Kick Counting:** Refer to page 204 for instructions on how and when to perform this test.

☐ **Sleep Questionnaire:** If you're feeling very tired, take the Pregnancy Sleep Risk Assessment on page 196 to make sure you're not sleep deprived.

Baby Milestones Five bony plates, joined by fibrous cartilage, make up the skull. They are not yet fused so that they can squeeze together during delivery, elongating the head, a phenomenon called *molding* (don't worry, this will resolve within a week or so after birth). Babies born by cesarean section or that don't sit in the pelvis very long will have a round head at birth.

Keeping Fit Aim for five 30- to 45-minute sessions a week.

ACTIVITY	MONDAY	TUESDAY	WEDNESDAY	THURSDAY	FRIDAY	SATURDAY	SUNDAY
walking/ aerobic exercise							
yoga/ stretching							
strength training							

Journaling Date _____

How do you feel about asking friends and family for help after your baby comes home?

_____
_____
_____
_____
_____
_____
_____
_____
_____
_____
_____
_____

How do you plan to deal with too many visitors after your baby is born?

_____

_____

_____

_____

_____

_____

_____

_____

Think about how you'd like your partner to help you out in the hospital and at home, for example, doing a late-night bottle feeding.

_____

_____

_____

_____

_____

_____

_____

_____

_____

_____

_____

_____

THE 37TH WEEK marks the point when you're considered at term. If you go into labor now, your baby will not be considered premature. In addition to your pelvic exam, you may also have an ultrasound to determine the volume of the amniotic fluid or a non-stress test, which measures your baby's heartbeat at rest and while moving to assess your baby's general well-being.

Here are some suggested questions to ask your practitioner:

What birth control method do you recommend after I've delivered?

When should I start?

When will I be able to exercise after the delivery?

If I have a cesarean section, what limitations will I have after the birth and for how long?

137

Notes for the
Twelfth Prenatal Visit (week 37)

Date _____

SYMPTOMS Write down any symptoms you have to discuss with your doctor, and then describe her response.

Symptoms

MD's response

YOUR RESULTS

Your weight _____

Blood pressure _____

Urine test for sugar _____

Urine test for protein _____

Fetal heart rate _____

Fundal height _____

Pelvic exam _____

**Notes for the
Thirteenth Prenatal Visit (week 38)**   Date _____

**SYMPTOMS Write down any symptoms you have to discuss with your doctor,
and then describe her response.**

Symptoms   MD's response

_____   _____

_____   _____

_____   _____

_____   _____

YOUR RESULTS

Your weight _____

Blood pressure _____

Urine test for sugar _____

Urine test for protein _____

Fetal heart rate _____

Fundal height _____

Pelvic exam _____

week 37

Symptom Soother: Poor Sleep A good night's sleep is becoming more difficult. You may wake up three to five times per night due to various late-night symptoms like leg cramps, heartburn, bladder discomfort, or backache. Make sure to avoid caffeine after lunch, use a body pillow for support, straighten your legs and flex your feet before going to bed, and avoid large evening meals.

How Long Until Labor

To get an idea when you'll need to pack your bags, take the How Long Until Labor questionnaire on page 205. Take it every two to three days, if you like, until your delivery.

Reminder

☐ **Aches and Pain Index:** If you are still experiencing pain, take Aches and Pain Index on page 203.

☐ **Kick Counting:** Refer to page 204 for instructions.

☐ **Mood Questionnaire:** See how your score compares with previous weeks, page 198.

Baby Milestones

Your baby is becoming aware of his environment, gathering information in the brain while awake, and storing it while asleep. This week he will recognize and turn his head toward a light. He is continuing to fill out with fat and the skin is pinker. His fingers are now strong and coordinated enough to grasp.

Important If exercise is becoming difficult or uncomfortable, don't push yourself. Limit your exercise to gentle walking.

Keeping Fit Aim for three to five 30- to 45-minute sessions a week. Whatever exercise you do at this point is helpful.

ACTIVITY	MONDAY	TUESDAY	WEDNESDAY	THURSDAY	FRIDAY	SATURDAY	SUNDAY
walking/ aerobic exercise							
yoga/ stretching							
strength training							

Journaling   Date _____

Write a letter to your unborn child, describing how you feel about his fast-approaching birth and having him join your family.

_____

_____

_____

_____

_____

_____

_____

_____

_____

_____

_____

_____

Pregnancy Pointer Ninety-five percent of women give birth within two weeks of their delivery date. During this holding pattern you probably won't continue to gain weight (you might even lose some). You might, though, feel more irritable—fed up with being uncomfortable and ready to have your baby.

!

Important Some hard plastic bottles contain a chemical plasticizer called Bisphenol-A. When heated, this chemical can leach from bottles (old, cracked, or scratched bottles leach the most). Since you'll want to do everything possible to keep your baby healthy, purchase glass bottles or choose plastic bottles that don't contain Bisphenol-A such as Medela brand bottles.

Reminder
☐ **How Long Until Labor?** Take the labor questionnaire on page 205 to determine how close you are to labor. Take every two to three days until your delivery.

☐ **Kick Counting:** Refer to page 204 for instructions on how and when to perform this test.

Baby Milestones
Your baby is now spending nearly 80 percent of her time in a deep sleep or in REM dreaming. The continued rapid growth and development of nerves throughout the brain is influenced by estradiol, one of the most potent hormonal triggers of brain cell growth. Your baby will be born with approximately seventy automatic reflexes.

Keeping Fit Aim for three to five 30- to 45-minute sessions a week.

ACTIVITY	MONDAY	TUESDAY	WEDNESDAY	THURSDAY	FRIDAY	SATURDAY	SUNDAY
walking/ aerobic exercise							
yoga/ stretching							
strength training							

Journaling   Date _____

Freewrite on the following pages about anything that comes to mind.

_____
_____
_____
_____
_____
_____
_____
_____
_____
_____
_____
_____
_____
_____

THESE VISITS will be very similar to your prior ones, with a pelvic exam and possibly an ultrasound.

Here are some suggested questions to ask your practitioner:

If my labor needs a jump-start, what methods or medications do you recommend?

What can I expect when my water breaks?

Are you in town during the next few weeks or have a vacation planned?

Has my cervix begun changing in preparation for labor?

Notes for the
Fourteenth Prenatal Visit (week 39)

Date _____

SYMPTOMS Write down any symptoms you have to discuss with your doctor, and then describe her response.

145

Symptoms

MD's response

_____   _____

_____   _____

_____   _____

_____   _____

_____   _____

_____   _____

_____   _____

_____   _____

_____   _____

YOUR RESULTS

Your weight _____

Blood pressure _____

Urine test for sugar _____

Urine test for protein _____

Fetal heart rate _____

Fundal height _____

Pelvic exam _____

Notes for the   Date _____
Fifteenth Prenatal Visit (week 40)

SYMPTOMS Write down any symptoms you have to discuss with your doctor,
and then describe her response.

Symptoms   MD's response

_____   _____

_____   _____

_____   _____

_____   _____

YOUR RESULTS

Your weight _____

Blood pressure _____

Urine test for sugar _____

Urine test for protein _____

Fetal heart rate _____

Fundal height _____

Pelvic exam _____

week

39

Pregnancy Pointer A few days to a week before delivery, you'll probably feel a burst of energy. Try not to overexert yourself and clean out all your closets. You might take advantage of this energy to buy some last-minute items like diapers, baby socks, or things you need to baby-proof your house—your newborn will be crawling before you know it.

Stress Relief Tip Visualization is a proven method for reducing stress. As you await your delivery, pick up a book on infant massage or watch a video. Look at the pictures, then close your eyes and visualize massaging, caressing, and bonding with your newborn.

Reminder
☐ **How Long Until Labor?** Take the labor questionnaire on page 205 to determine how close you are to labor. Take every two to three days until your delivery.
☐ **Kick Counting:** Refer to page 204 for instructions on how and when to perform this test.

Baby Milestones
Your baby does not have tear ducts yet—they will appear within a few weeks after birth, yet his eyes are fully developed and can focus perfectly on objects 8 to 12 inches away.

! **Important** If you have a tattoo on your lower back in the area where you would get an epidural or spinal injection for pain during labor, you will need to plan ahead. Ink from the tattoo can accidentally get injected into the spinal fluid. Talk to your doctor in advance, as the anesthesiologist will need to use a special type of catheter with a "stylet," which may not be routinely stocked in your hospital.

Keeping Fit Aim for three to five 30- to 45-minute sessions a week.

ACTIVITY	MONDAY	TUESDAY	WEDNESDAY	THURSDAY	FRIDAY	SATURDAY	SUNDAY
walking/ aerobic exercise							
yoga/ stretching							
strength training							

Journaling   Date _____

What do you think are the most important traits parents should have, and how will you try to fulfill them?

_____

_____

_____

_____

_____

_____

_____

_____

_____

_____

_____

Write about the traits that you and your partner have (great sense of humor, compassion, musical talent) that you'd like to be sure to bestow to your child, and think about ways to accomplish that.

_____

_____

_____

_____

_____

_____

_____

_____

_____

_____

_____

149

What family traditions would you like to continue, and what new ones would you like to establish?

_____

_____

_____

_____

_____

_____

_____

_____

_____

week
40

Pregnancy Pointer You might be wondering about what or who triggers labor. Is it your baby sending out signals that she's ready to greet the world? Is it your body and brain, signaling that enough is enough? In fact, labor is set off by a number of conditions and hormonal signals coming from you, your baby, and the placenta. It's not known whether there is one triggering event or several. If you want to add your two cents and try to get a move on labor, some safe but not necessarily reliable methods are having sex, walking, or eating spicy foods. Caveat: Don't use herbal labor-inducers, which may be harmful.

Stress Relief Tip If you plan to breast-feed, request a referral for a lactation consultant. Breast-feeding might feel uncomfortable, and may even be frustrating. Having the name of someone who can help you when you get home from the hospital may relieve any anxiety surrounding it.

150

Reminder
☐ **How Long Until Labor?** Take the questionnaire on page 205 to see how close you are to labor. Take every two to three days until your delivery.

☐ **Aches and Pain Index:** Take this test if you're experiencing pain. Refer to page 203.

☐ **Kick Counting:** Count kicks whenever you are concerned or think you haven't felt a kick for a while. Refer to page 204 for instructions on how and when to perform this test.

Baby Milestones
At birth your baby's brain will have about 100 billion primed and ready-to-learn nerve cells, or neurons, about as many as an adult. She will have two soft spots, or *fontanels,* on the top of her skull, one toward the front and a smaller one toward the back, where the bones of the skull have not yet come together. The small fontanel will completely close by the twelfth week of life and the larger one by the eighteenth month.

Keeping Fit Aim for three to five 30- to 45-minute sessions a week.

ACTIVITY	MONDAY	TUESDAY	WEDNESDAY	THURSDAY	FRIDAY	SATURDAY	SUNDAY
walking/ aerobic exercise							
yoga/ stretching							
strength training							

Journaling   Date _____

If you haven't delivered yet, write about how uncomfortable you feel.

_____

_____

_____

_____

_____

_____

_____

_____

_____

_____

_____

_____

Have you thought of trying or tried any labor inducing tactics?

IF YOU HAVEN'T delivered by your due date, you might be concerned. Rest assured your due date is just an estimation. However, if you are one week post-date, your practitioner will monitor you and your baby closely to make sure the aging placenta is able to continue providing the oxygen and nutrients your baby needs. She might begin to measure your baby's health twice a week with an electronic fetal monitor. She might also recommend an ultrasound to measure the amniotic fluid around your baby and to measure your baby's movement, called a biophysical profile.

Here are some suggested questions to ask your practitioner:

Do you recommend a biophysical profile?

What limitations do you recommend I place on my activity?

Is my cervix dilating or softening?

Has the baby descended into my pelvis?

Notes for the Sixteenth Prenatal Visit (week 41)

Date _____

SYMPTOMS Write down any symptoms you have to discuss with your doctor, and then describe her response.

Symptoms

MD's response

_____   _____

_____   _____

_____   _____

_____   _____

_____   _____

_____   _____

_____   _____

YOUR RESULTS

Your weight _____

Blood pressure _____

Urine test for sugar _____

Urine test for protein _____

Fetal heart rate _____

Fundal height _____

Pelvic exam _____

Notes for the
Seventeenth Prenatal Visit (week 42)

Date _____

SYMPTOMS Write down any symptoms you have to discuss with your doctor, and then describe her response.

Symptoms

MD's response

_____   _____

_____   _____

_____   _____

_____   _____

YOUR RESULTS

Your weight _____

Blood pressure _____

Urine test for sugar _____

Urine test for protein _____

Fetal heart rate _____

Fundal height _____

Pelvic exam _____

weeks 41 & 42 (Post Due Date)

Pregnancy Pointer

About 5 percent of pregnancies go beyond their due date. Your practitioner might recommend you closely monitor kick counts at home. If you go two weeks beyond your due date, your practitioner will probably decide to induce your labor (if your cervix is ready) or schedule a cesarean section.

Reminder

☐ **How Long Until Labor?** Take the questionnaire on page 205 to see how close you are to labor. Take every two to three days until your delivery.

☐ **Kick Counting** Count kicks whenever you are concerned or think you haven't felt a kick for a while. Refer to page 204 for instructions on how and when to perform this test.

Keeping Fit Talk to your healthcare provider about safe exercise recommendations.

ACTIVITY	MONDAY	TUESDAY	WEDNESDAY	THURSDAY	FRIDAY	SATURDAY	SUNDAY
walking/ aerobic exercise							
yoga/ stretching							
strength training							

As your due date passes, there's a lot to grumble about. Put your thoughts down on paper.

_____

_____

_____

_____

_____

_____

_____

_____

_____

Write about any concerns you have about your post-due-date option—waiting it out, inducing labor, or having a cesarean section.

_____

_____

_____

_____

_____

_____

_____

_____

_____

_____

_____

_____

IT MIGHT BE EARLY in your pregnancy when you glance at these labor and delivery pages. Many women begin thinking about the big event soon after they get pregnant. Educating yourself about childbirth is the best way to ease any anxieties you may have, and being as prepared as possible for your delivery can help it proceed more smoothly.

How can you tell if you are in labor?

TRUE VERSUS FALSE LABOR

You are probably in labor if contractions . . .	It is probably a false alarm if contractions . . .
are persistent	come and go
begin in lower back and move to abdomen	are felt in lower abdomen and pelvis
become more frequent and persistent	do not change in frequency or intensity
often become more frequent with walking	are not affected by walking
are associated with "water breaking" or ruptured membranes	are not associated with water breaking

What happens during labor?

Labor has three phases. **Early labor** averages about 6 to 12 hours for first-time moms. During this phase contractions occur every 5 to 30 minutes and your cervix dilates from 0 to 4 centimeters. Most women are told to go to their hospital or birthing center when contractions come every five minutes. The second phase, **active labor**, lasts about 3 to 6 hours as your cervix dilates from 4 to 6 centimeters. Contractions during this phase occur every 3 minutes and may last 45 to 60 seconds. **Transition** is the final stage when your cervix completely dilates from 6 to 10 centimeters. This last stage is the most intense and takes anywhere from 10 minutes to two hours.

What happens during delivery?

Once your cervix is fully dilated you can begin to push. Moving your baby through the birth canal can take a few minutes or a few hours. Your labor coach or delivery team will tell you when to push through your contractions. You'll rest in between contractions. After your baby is born, you'll also have to "deliver" the placenta, and your doctor will repair any tears or cuts to your perineum, the area surrounding the opening of the birth canal.

What can I do to improve my comfort during labor?

EARLY LABOR COMFORT MEASURES

Walk

Rock in a chair

Take a warm shower or bath
(unless your water has broken)

Take a nap if possible

Suck on Popsicles

Read a magazine or watch a movie

Use aromatherapy with lavender
or clary sage

ACTIVE LABOR COMFORT MEASURES

Walk or rock as long as your practitioner
gives the okay

Take slow deep breaths

Take a warm shower if permitted

Request pain medication if and when you
are ready

Ask for firm low back massage or pressure

Listen to soothing music

Use lip moisturizer

Use aromatherapy

TRANSITION COMFORT MEASURES

Cool compresses to forehead

Change position frequently

What do I bring to the hospital or birthing center?

When preparing your hospital bag, include these useful items:

LABOR

☐ Birth plan

☐ Lip moisturizer

☐ Hard candy

☐ Hair tie

☐ Favorite pillow

☐ CD or MP3 player and favorite
   music

☐ Socks and slippers

POST DELIVERY

☐ Supportive nursing bra or support bra
   if not nursing

☐ Nightgown and several changes of
   underwear

☐ Deodorant, toothbrush, toothpaste,
   and hairbrush

☐ Breast pads for leaky breasts

☐ List of phone numbers of people
   to call

☐ Camera

Anything personal you would like to add to your bag:

_____

_____

_____

_____

A Record of Your Labor and Delivery

What day did you go into labor?

_____

_____

What were you doing when you went into labor?

_____

_____

_____

How would you describe your contractions and how did they compare to your expectations?

_____

_____

_____

_____

How did your labor progress?

_____

_____

_____

_____

159

Who delivered your baby?

_____

_____

Who was with you when your baby was born?

_____

_____

_____

Are there any special nurses you wish to remember?

_____

_____

_____

What date and time did you deliver?

_____

_____

Your Baby's Vital Statistics

Baby's name: _____

Weight _____ Length _____ Apgar scores _____

Additional Notes

_____

_____

_____

_____

_____

_____

_____

POSTPARTUM

1 to 12 weeks

THE THREE MONTHS AFTER childbirth can be as joyous as they are challenging. You may have incredible feelings of maternal love and nurturing toward your newborn, but your resources may be depleted in the first few days after your labor and delivery—or even longer if you've had a cesarean section. Add to the emotional and physical mix, the plummet in your pregnancy hormones and sleep deprivation due to the dusk-to-dawn feedings and you may be feeling moody or blue or worse. During the next year, it's important to be on the lookout for signs of depression. Postpartum >

depression is not uncommon. It can affect your quality
of life and your health, and it can be harmful to your
baby's development.

In the first few weeks of life, your newborn baby
sleeps, eats, gazes, and goes through many a diaper.
But just a few weeks later, he's winning you over with
smiles and coos. His brain is developing at rapid-fire
pace, and responding to the stimulation he gets.
Though your main focus will be on meeting his very
basic needs, keeping him engaged and stimulated when
awake can enhance his early developmental stages.

week

1

Postpartum Pointer Many new moms experience the *baby blues* around the third day after delivery. This is a brief depression, triggered by a plunge in the hormones estradiol and progesterone. It typically resolves within a week, but if feelings of sadness linger, it may be an indication of postpartum depression, a more serious condition that requires treatment. Other symptoms of postpartum depression include hopelessness, confusion, intense fatigue, or dramatic shifts in appetite. If postpartum depression is left untreated, your newborn will not get the stimulation from you that's needed for proper brain development and your own well-being will be compromised. Postpartum depression can occur anytime during the first year after delivery.

Breast-feeding Tip To simply maintain your weight while breast-feeding, you need to get an additional 400 to 500 calories per day over what you ate during your third trimester. If you want to lose weight, you still need to increase your calories, but not quite as much.

161

Symptom Soother: Sore Breasts Two to four days after you deliver, your milk will come in and your breasts may become engorged. The fullness and tightness can be uncomfortable. Make sure you wear a good support bra. If you are breast-feeding, try to nurse every two hours during the day and every three hours at night for 10 to 15 minutes on each side. If your nipples flatten, manually express or gently pump enough milk to allow your baby to latch on properly. If your baby is having difficulty nursing or your breasts are still engorged after you nurse, pump for 5 to 10 minutes or until your breasts are soft. If you are not breast-feeding, avoid stimulating your breasts and use ice packs to ease the swelling. Hang in there; engorgement should subside after about 36 to 48 hours.

Stress Relief Tip Dreams during the postpartum period—if you ever get enough sleep to fall into a REM state—may involve delivery scenarios or your baby being harmed. Try to write your dreams down the minute you wake up.

The Benefits of Breast-feeding

The benefits of breast-feeding have been well established, though not all women choose or are able to nurse. The American Academy of Pediatrics encourages you to exclusively breast-feed for the first six months of your baby's life, and continue to nurse with some supplemented food until your baby's first birthday.

Here are some of the benefits of breast-feeding for you and your baby.

FOR BABY	FOR MOM
Lower risk of infections	Reduction in postpartum bleeding
Lower risk of food allergies and asthma	Stress relief
Higher IQ	Lower risk of depression
Better adjusted children	Lower rate of anemia
Lower risk of diabetes	Lower risk of diabetes
Lower risk of leukemia	Lower risk of breast and ovarian cancer
Lower risk of childhood obesity	Stronger bones
Unique health benefits for premature babies	Less expense

Baby Milestones

Nearly 75 percent of the growth and development of your baby's brain takes place after delivery. New neural connections in the brain are forming at a rate of three billion per second. Each new experience stimulates these connections and lays down memories. This first month is critical for processing sensory information. Your newborn recognizes your voice and smell immediately after birth and already has taste preferences. She can see objects that are 12 to 18 inches away. She prefers to gaze upon your face, and may even start to mimic your facial expressions. Try sticking your tongue out slowly or opening your mouth wide to see if she tries to imitate you. She can only see black and white (her color vision comes in at month four), so don't pull out the pastels just yet.

Journaling

Date _____

Describe how your labor and delivery went and how it compared to what you expected, and journal about what went well and any disappointments you felt.

_____

_____

_____

_____

_____

_____

_____

_____

_____

_____

_____

_____

_____

_____

_____

_____

_____

_____

_____

_____

_____

_____

_____

week 2

Postpartum Pointer If you had an uncomplicated vaginal delivery, you can start a walking program as soon as you recover from childbirth and feel up to it. Start out slowly, and gradually increase your intensity. Stop if you have any pain. It takes your body about four to six weeks to shift from a pregnant to nonpregnant state, so be easy on yourself. Your joints are still malleable, and you may lack balance and coordination because of your low estradiol level. Do not resume yoga until three weeks after delivery.

Breast-feeding Tip To provide healthy milk for your newborn, continue to eat organic foods whenever possible and avoid eating unhealthy fats, particularly trans fats, found in commercially baked products and French fries. These are easily passed on through your breast milk.

Important Continue taking your prenatal vitamins for three to six months after you deliver, to make sure you are getting all the nutrients you need, whether you are breast-feeding or bottle-feeding.

Healthy Eating Approximately 60 percent of your baby's brain and nerves are made of healthy fats. The omega-3 fatty acid DHA is particularly crucial for proper brain functioning and development. During your baby's first year of life, his brain will triple in size. Growing brains need DHA. If you are breast-feeding, your milk naturally contains DHA, though levels vary significantly depending on your diet. To ensure your baby's brain gets enough DHA, continue taking your DHA supplement like Expecta LIPIL. If you are bottle-feeding, use formula supplemented with DHA.

Mood Questionnaire
It's important to carefully monitor your mood to make sure your baby blues don't evolve into a postpartum depression. Take the mood questionnaire on page 198.

Stress Relief Tip You may have the expectation that being a new mom would bring you great happiness. If negative thoughts, such as feeling overwhelmed or not bonding immediately with your baby creep in, they can lead to feelings of guilt. Rest assured, these are normal emotions and don't necessarily mean you're depressed—or that you're a bad mom. Use the journaling page this week to put these thoughts down on paper; it will help relieve any stress surrounding these feelings.

 Baby Milestones
Your newborn has his first growth spurt at about 7 to 10 days after birth. You may notice a heightened hunger and more frequent cries for milk. During his first month, he starts to respond to sounds with a blink, a startle, or a frown.

Sleep wake cycles vary considerably, but in general, newborns sleep between feedings (if not dozing off mid-feeding). Hiccups, especially after eating, are adorable—and normal. He may also sneeze a lot to clear mucous and dust from his nose.

Keeping Fit Aim for five 30- to 45-minute sessions a week.

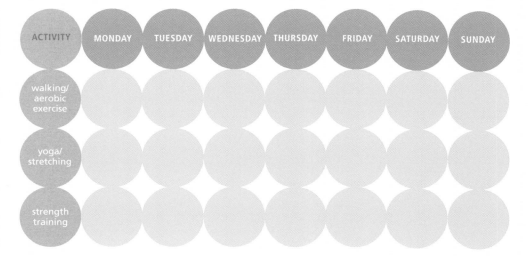

ACTIVITY	MONDAY	TUESDAY	WEDNESDAY	THURSDAY	FRIDAY	SATURDAY	SUNDAY
walking/ aerobic exercise							
yoga/ stretching							
strength training							

Journaling

Date _____

Freewrite about any emotions you're experiencing—whether positive or nega-tive (remember that this journal is for your eyes only).

_____

_____

_____

_____

_____

_____

_____

_____

_____

_____

_____

_____

_____

_____

_____

_____

_____

_____

_____

_____

_____

_____

IF YOU HAD a cesarean section, you will probably see your doctor this week for a general exam. She will examine your breasts and your incision and evaluate your vaginal bleeding. If your score on the Mood Questionnaire concerns you, discuss the results with your physician. If your doctor downplays or trivializes your concerns about your state of mind, be your own advocate and ask her why she isn't taking your concerns seriously. Postpartum depression is now widely recognized as a serious medical condition that can impact your health as well as your baby's continued brain development. Obstetricians, pediatricians, and family physicians are all being urged to diagnose and treat this condition.

Here are some suggested questions to ask your healthcare provider:

When can I drive?

Are there any other restrictions?

Is there anything that can help speed my recovery?

When can I start to exercise and how hard can I work out?

Can we review my birth control options?

167

Notes for this **Postpartum Visit**   Date _____

SYMPTOMS Write down any symptoms you have to discuss with your doctor, and then describe her response.

Symptoms

MD's response

_____

_____

_____

_____

_____

_____

_____

_____

YOUR RESULTS (the following tests might be part of your postpartum care).

Your weight _____   Blood pressure _____

Blood test for anemia _____

week

3

Postpartum Pointer Most women lose about 12 to 14 pounds immediately following the birth of their baby. The rest of your weight will come off more slowly, and it can take about nine months to get back to your prepregnancy weight—that's if you maintain a healthy diet and get regular exercise. For the normal weight woman (see chart in week 10, page 39) who gains 25 pounds during pregnancy, aim to lose about 1 to 3 pounds a month. The longer you breast-feed, the more likely you are to lose excess fat.

Breast-feeding Tip If you are concerned that your baby is not getting enough milk, make sure he nurses at least ten times a day and wets six diapers a day. If he acts content and happy, he is probably getting enough.

Baby Milestones
Your newborn might experience a second growth spurt this week and may seem more hungry or fussy. Your baby learns language through interactions, and responds best to high-pitched "baby talk." Until the cerebral cortex, the area of the brain that receives sensory stimulation, matures between the second to fourth month, tone down the pace and intensity of your interactions. This is even more important if you sense your baby becoming overwhelmed.

Fatigue Assessment Calendar
Your day-to-day strength and energy should steadily improve through the postpartum period. To be sure you're recovering, fill out the daily month-long Fatigue Assessment Calendar on page 208. Be sure to make an entry every day. If you're not seeing a trend toward better health and energy, talk to your healthcare provider.

Post-Traumatic Stress Disorder Screening
If you frequently have negative thoughts or think about a bad incident in the past or have nightmares, there's a chance that you are suffering from post-traumatic stress disorder (PTSD). The dramatic drop in hormones that occurs postpartum can make you more susceptible to PTSD, and having a traumatic delivery or emergency cesarean section can trigger it. Take the PTSD Screening Questionnaire on page 207 to help evaluate whether you may be suffering from this disorder.

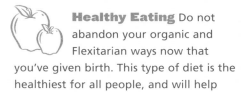

Healthy Eating Do not abandon your organic and Flexitarian ways now that you've given birth. This type of diet is the healthiest for all people, and will help keep your hormones balanced as you lose your pregnancy weight. Also, it's the type of diet you'll want your children to follow, so lead by example.

Keeping Fit Aim for five 30- to 45-minute sessions a week.

ACTIVITY	MONDAY	TUESDAY	WEDNESDAY	THURSDAY	FRIDAY	SATURDAY	SUNDAY
walking/ aerobic exercise							
yoga/ stretching							
strength training							

169

Journaling   Date _____

Describe your first night home with your baby.

_____

_____

_____

_____

_____

_____

_____

Describe your level of satisfaction with the help and support you're getting.

How are you coping with company and visitors?

week 4

Healthy Eating New moms have a small risk of anemia and the accompanying fatigue due to the loss of blood that occurs during delivery. Make sure you are getting enough iron each day:

Eat foods rich in iron (see week 32 for suggestions).

Take a supplement containing 125 mg or a prenatal vitamin with iron.

Eat foods high in vitamin C.

Symptom Soother: Sleep Deprivation

Late-night feedings can rob you of deep restorative sleep. Even if your new-mom adrenaline is making it hard to take a nap, you need to catch up on your sleep. Sleep deprivation can affect your judgment and moods. Try to get one six-hour stretch of sleep by asking your partner to do one late night or early morning feeding. Try to take a 20- to 25-minute nap during midafternoon—when your body's circadian rhythm is slowing down so you'll be more likely to nod off.

171

Reminder

☐ Fatigue Assessment Calendar: page 208. Be sure to make an entry every day.

Baby Milestones

Your baby loves eye contact. Exaggerated facial expressions are a great way to engage your baby in face-to-face play. She is starting to experiment with different cries for hunger versus cries for frustration or pain. The tone, urgency, and pitch or the time of day will help you decode her cries. This is an important step in verbal communication but it's a learning process. By now she is nearly able to distinguish between syllables that sound similar such as "me" and "be." And she should soon be able to lift her head very briefly and turn it from side to side when on her tummy.

Stress Relief Tip Join a new moms support group. You'll get together with a handful of brand-new moms and talk about your lack of sleep, breast-feeding, crying, gas, husbands, and all other pertinent issues. The commiseration will help normalize your experience, and you can walk away with some helpful advice from other moms. To locate one, call your hospital or birthing center, check out mothering networks, local Web sites, and yoga studios or gyms where postnatal classes are offered.

Keeping Fit Aim for five 30- to 45-minute sessions a week.

ACTIVITY	MONDAY	TUESDAY	WEDNESDAY	THURSDAY	FRIDAY	SATURDAY	SUNDAY
walking/ aerobic exercise							
yoga/ stretching							
strength training							

Journaling Date _____

Freewrite about whatever comes to mind.

_____

_____

_____

_____

_____

_____

week

5

Postpartum Pointer Resuming your sex life after delivery can be challenging for some. Your hormones are still low, putting a damper on your libido for weeks or months following delivery. Being sleep-deprived may also cool your interest in sex for both you and your partner. Sex might also be painful because the lack of estradiol can reduce lubrication. Try not to stress out about it as your sex life will probably resume soon, though it may be different than it was prechildren. For now use lubrication, take a brisk late-afternoon walk, which will dilate blood vessels to the vagina for hours, or use alternatives to intercourse. Talk to your practitioner about treatment if sexual issues do not "normalize" within three to six months.

Breast-feeding Tip If you are having any difficulties with breast-feeding, like low milk supply, call a lactation consultant. Often hospital lactation specialists leave you their card in case you have trouble. You can also call your pediatrician or consider speaking with a representative from the local chapter of LaLeche League.

Baby Milestones
The second month is a critical period for your baby to experience basic emotions like being happy or sad. He is learning that crying gets a response from you and your response reinforces that the world is a safe place. He also starts to focus both eyes on an object at the same time and track its movement.

Stress-Relief Tip Staying home with your baby may leave you feeling socially isolated. Get out of the house together—take the stroller to local parks and playgrounds or into town. Also try to have some baby-free activities, like getting together with friends, going to a gym or yoga class, or joining a local group that offers moms night-out activities.

Reminder
☐ Fatigue Assessment Calendar: page 208. Be sure to make an entry every day.

Keeping Fit Aim for five 30- to 45-minute sessions a week.

ACTIVITY	MONDAY	TUESDAY	WEDNESDAY	THURSDAY	FRIDAY	SATURDAY	SUNDAY
walking/ aerobic exercise							
yoga/ stretching							
strength training							

Journaling

Date _____

Write about your thoughts on going back to work or any thoughts you have about staying home if you're taking a break from the career track.

_____

_____

_____

_____

_____

_____

_____

_____

_____

_____

_____

_____

_____

week 6

Postpartum Pointer There have been sporadic news reports implicating certain foods a breast-feeding woman eats with an increased risk of allergies in her baby. These risks have been over-hyped as there's no good evidence that early exposure through a mother's milk increases a child's risk of allergies. It's not necessary to avoid known allergens, except for peanuts if you or your partner has a personal or family history of food allergies. Discuss your concerns with your pediatrician. The American Academy of Pediatrics recommends not introducing your baby to solid foods until she is six months old.

Breast-feeding Tip You'll hear a lot of breast-feeding advice, but much of it is based on old wives' tales and anecdotes rather than on science. To do some myth-busting: garlic has not been shown to cause newborns discomfort, and beer, wine, and coffee have not been shown to increase milk supply. Spacing out feedings to allow your breasts time to fill up does not improve milk production and may have the opposite effect. But your milk supply *can* be improved by breast-feeding your baby frequently, on demand.

177

Reminder
☐ Mood Questionnaire: Take the mood questionnaire on page 198 and see how it compares to your previous score from postpartum week 2.
☐ Fatigue Assessment Calendar: page 208. Be sure to make an entry every day.

Baby Milestones
A third growth spurt might occur this week. Your baby will begin smiling, cooing, or blowing bubbles when you play together. His hands now touch and explore different textures; soft toys bring the most pleasure. His movements will become more deliberate and he will start to hold his head up for longer periods of time when on his tummy.

Stress Relief Tip Schedule a few hours at the spa or beauty salon or get a massage. You deserve a special relaxing new-mom treat.

Keeping Fit Aim for five 30- to 45-minute sessions a week.

ACTIVITY	MONDAY	TUESDAY	WEDNESDAY	THURSDAY	FRIDAY	SATURDAY	SUNDAY
walking/ aerobic exercise							
yoga/ stretching							
strength training							

Journaling   Date _____

Have you experienced any emotions you did not expect since delivering?

_____

_____

_____

_____

_____

_____

_____

_____

_____

_____

_____

_____

_____

_____

Write about your efforts to get out of the house and meet other new moms. Have you been getting enough adult contact?

IF YOU HAD an uncomplicated vaginal delivery, you will probably see your doctor this week for a general exam. She will examine your breasts and your perineum, the area surrounding the birth canal, for tears, and she'll examine your episiotomy if you had one. Your physician may recommend a pap smear if you are due. She'll also evaluate any vaginal bleeding. If your score on the Mood Questionnaire concerns you, be sure to discuss the results with your physician. If your doctor downplays or trivializes your concerns about your state of mind, be your own advocate and ask her why she isn't taking your concerns seriously.

Here are some suggested questions to ask your healthcare provider:

Can we review my birth control options?

When can I start a weight loss program?

When can I start to exercise and what level is safe?

When can we resume sexual intercourse?

180

Notes for the **Postpartum Visit**   Date _____

SYMPTOMS Write down any symptoms you have to discuss with your doctor, and then describe her response.

Symptoms

MD's response

_____ _____

_____ _____

_____ _____

_____ _____

_____ _____

_____ _____

YOUR RESULTS (the following tests might be part of your postpartum care.)

Your weight _____   Blood pressure _____

Blood test for anemia _____

week 7

Stress Relief Tip You're halfway to the three-month milestone, at which point your baby will settle into a respectable sleep-wake pattern, need less round-the-clock attention, and start to be playful. The rewards and joy of a bouncing, grinning, and happy baby will soon start pouring in.

Bladder Symptom Questionnaire If you're experiencing frequent urination, an urgency to urinate, or discomfort with sex, take the bladder questionnaire on page 212 to see if you may be suffering from painful bladder syndrome. You may need to seek treatment or reevaluate the treatment regimen you are currently on. Take this once a week as long as your symptoms persist to determine whether your symptoms are worsening and might need treatment.

Keeping Fit Aim for five 30- to 45-minute sessions a week.

ACTIVITY	MONDAY	TUESDAY	WEDNESDAY	THURSDAY	FRIDAY	SATURDAY	SUNDAY
walking/ aerobic exercise							
yoga/ stretching							
strength training							

Baby Milestones
By now, you may start to understand your baby's unique temperament. This will help guide your interactions and the type of play and stimulation your baby prefers.

Your newborn might appreciate being placed on a blanket on the floor with plenty of room to stretch and kick those arms and legs. Fly a shiny helium balloon above her to visually stimulate her. It might even elicit her first genuine smile.

Freewrite on the topic of your support system, thinking about how supportive
your partner and other family members are and what they can do to help you.

week 8

Symptom Soother: Low Back Pain

Your back may still be recovering from your pregnancy posture, and as a new mom, you may endure some new insults to it, such as hunching over a changing table or bassinet, carrying the baby in a car seat, pushing strollers, or taking walks with a baby carrier. It's important to maintain good posture and to lift by bending at the knees, not the waist. To prevent pain, try walking and do exercises to strengthen your back and abdomen.

Breast-feeding Tip If you are pumping your breast milk or if you have to return to work, use the following tips to store your milk:

1 HOUR at room temperature. After that, toss it. Try to refrigerate or freeze your milk as soon as you can after pumping.

2 DAYS in the refrigerator (40°F or below). After that, dump it. Don't store milk on the refrigerator door as the temperature can vary there.

3 MONTHS in the freezer (0°F or below). This is the longest it can be frozen without losing vital nutrients. Don't thaw breast milk at room temperature. Instead run it under warm tap water until it thaws to body temperature. Then use it immediately and discard whatever is left.

Baby Milestones

Your baby can now track moving objects up to 180 degrees and is starting to reach for objects with his hands that now open and close purposefully. He is beginning to associate your moving lips with words. Now's the time to introduce a bedtime routine. Singing, reading, rocking, or cuddling are all wonderful bedtime soothers.

Stress Relief Tip

Postpartum yoga can help you feel relaxed and rejuvenated. A 30-minute session can also reduce stress hormone levels by up to 80 percent. If you don't have 30 minutes, break it up into three 10-minute sessions and place your baby in front of you on a blanket. As an alternative, take a mommy-and-me yoga class or spend 15 minutes stretching.

Reminder

☐ Bladder Symptom Questionnaire: If you're still having urinary problems or discomfort with sex, take the bladder questionnaire on page 212.

Keeping Fit Aim for five 30- to 45-minute sessions a week.

ACTIVITY	MONDAY	TUESDAY	WEDNESDAY	THURSDAY	FRIDAY	SATURDAY	SUNDAY
walking/ aerobic exercise							
yoga/ stretching							
strength training							

Journaling   Date _____

What has been the most striking or unexpected change in your life since you delivered?

_____

_____

_____

_____

_____

_____

_____

_____

_____

_____

_____

_____

_____

If this is your second (or third) baby, how are the siblings coping?

_____

_____

_____

_____

_____

_____

_____

_____

What are some ways you like to pamper yourself? Are you doing it?

_____

_____

_____

_____

_____

_____

_____

_____

_____

week 9

Postpartum Pointer If you're exclusively breast-feeding, you have a less than 2 percent chance of getting pregnant. But if you're also supplementing with baby formula, don't consider yourself protected. Many women avoid hormone contraceptives because they worry that the hormones will affect the baby and that estrogen will reduce milk production. One good solution is the NuvaRing, a combination estrogen and progestin, which has the lowest dose of all hormonal contraceptives, and is unlikely to affect your milk supply nor will it be passed in your milk to your baby. You can use this when you are three months postpartum. You insert this flexible ring into your vagina and leave it in for three weeks.

Reminder
☐ Bladder Symptom Questionnaire: If you're having urinary problems or discomfort with sex, take the bladder questionnaire on page 212.

Keeping Fit Aim for five 30- to 45-minute sessions a week.

ACTIVITY	MONDAY	TUESDAY	WEDNESDAY	THURSDAY	FRIDAY	SATURDAY	SUNDAY
walking/ aerobic exercise							
yoga/ stretching							
strength training							

Baby Milestones

As you reach the three-month mark, your baby will benefit from spending 5 to 10 minutes several times per day on her tummy when she's awake. Because babies are now put to bed on their backs to help prevent SIDS (Sudden Infant Death Syndrome), they need to spend awake time on their tummy to strengthen their neck, body, and arms for crawling. Slowly increase tummy time as she gets used to it.

Journaling   Date _____

What changes have you seen in your husband?

_____

_____

_____

_____

What changes have you seen in your family dynamics?

_____

_____

_____

_____

_____

If you could have a "date night" with your partner, what would it be?

_____

_____

_____

_____

_____

week 10

Stress Relief Tip
Several studies have shown that 15 minutes of baby massage two or three times a week can reduce your baby's crying (a relief for you as well) and increase her awake time. Gentle massage can be used to ease your baby to sleep as effectively as rocking. Be careful to do it very softly and only after you've discussed this with your pediatrician and read up on baby massage techniques.

Reminder
☐ **Mood Questionnaire:** Take the mood questionnaire on page 198 and see how it compares to your previous scores.

☐ **Bladder Symptom Questionnaire:** If you're having urinary problems or discomfort with sex, take the bladder questionnaire on page 212.

! Important
When breastfeeding, you can produce up to 3 cups of milk per day. Get plenty of fluids to prevent dehydration.

Keeping Fit
Aim for five 30- to 45-minute sessions a week.

ACTIVITY	MONDAY	TUESDAY	WEDNESDAY	THURSDAY	FRIDAY	SATURDAY	SUNDAY
walking/ aerobic exercise							
yoga/ stretching							
strength training							

Baby Milestones

During the third month, your newborn will begin to distinguish words and process sounds.

Hold her upright on your lap; soon her feet will push off a surface as she practices using her legs and strengthens her muscles.

Journaling　　　　Date _____

Freewrite about whatever comes to mind.

IF YOU HAD a cesarean section, you will probably see your doctor this week for a follow-up exam. She will examine your breasts and your nearly healed incision. Again, if your score on the Mood Questionnaire concerns you, discuss the results with your physician and make sure she takes your concerns seriously.

Here are some suggested questions to ask your healthcare provider:

When can I start a weight loss program?

Can we resume sexual intercourse?

When will the redness of my scar fade and when will it stop tugging?

Since I had a cesarean section, will I be able to have a vaginal delivery with my next pregnancy?

Notes for the **Postpartum Visit**   Date _____

SYMPTOMS Write down any symptoms you have to discuss with your doctor, and then describe her response.

190

Symptoms

MD's response

_____   _____

_____   _____

_____   _____

_____   _____

_____   _____

_____   _____

_____   _____

YOUR RESULTS (the following tests might be part of your postpartum care).

Your weight _____   Blood pressure _____

Blood test for anemia _____

week 11

Postpartum Pointer During pregnancy, high levels of estrogen and testosterone made your hair look healthy and shiny. But the drop in these hormones after delivery takes a toll on your locks. You may notice an unusually large amount of hair in your brush or the shower drain around the third or fourth month after childbirth. This can be distressing, but in most cases your hair will return to normal by the sixth postpartum month. In the meantime, avoid hair-styles that pull your hair, and blow dry on a low heat setting. If it continues beyond that time or is falling out in patches, talk to your practitioner about testing for hypothyroidism or anemia, both of which can cause hair loss.

Reminder
☐ Bladder Symptom Questionnaire: page 212.

Keeping Fit Aim for five 30- to 45-minute sessions a week.

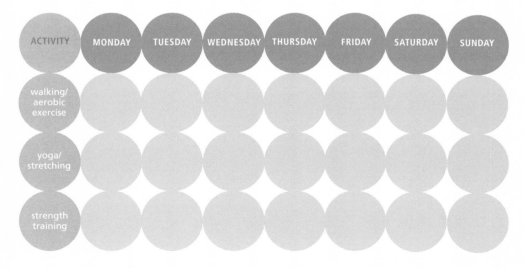

ACTIVITY	MONDAY	TUESDAY	WEDNESDAY	THURSDAY	FRIDAY	SATURDAY	SUNDAY
walking/ aerobic exercise							
yoga/ stretching							
strength training							

Baby Milestones
As your baby's brain matures, bright colors and sharply contrasting objects will provide the most stimulation. Your baby will begin to understand that objects, like balls, need to be manipulated in order to move.

Journaling   Date _____

What is your sex life like now; do you have any apprehensions or concerns?

_____

_____

_____

_____

_____

Has your partner's body changed? Is he losing weight too (recall Couvades syndrome)?

_____

_____

_____

_____

What is your favorite thing to do with your newborn?

_____

_____

_____

_____

_____

week 12

Postpartum Pointer

By the end of your third month, your hormones are beginning to stabilize, though it might take until you stop breast-feeding for them to fully return to your prepregnancy state. Up until then, continue to use the dietary advice in this journal, but once you stop nursing, consider following the program for all women in *Dr. Robert Greene's Perfect Balance*. It will help you lose your pregnancy weight and keep you feeling healthy and balanced. You'll find it has similar guidelines and suggestions to the program developed for pregnancy with unique troubleshooting tips that many women encounter from puberty through menopause. By taking steps to maintain your hormone balance, you'll feel better while you lower your risk of future health problems including any complications during your next pregnancy.

Reminder

☐ Bladder Symptom Questionnaire: If you're having urinary problems or discomfort with sex, take the bladder questionnaire on page 212.

Keeping Fit Aim for five 30- to 45-minute sessions a week.

ACTIVITY	MONDAY	TUESDAY	WEDNESDAY	THURSDAY	FRIDAY	SATURDAY	SUNDAY
walking/ aerobic exercise							
yoga/ stretching							
strength training							

Baby Milestones

Your baby may be in the midst of his fourth growth spurt. He is also starting to respond to you verbally with gurgles and is starting to sort out who's who. Soon he might smile at a stranger but when you enter the room, he'll wave his arms and kick his legs in excitement. He'll also start to swat at an object he wants.

Journaling

Date _____

Write a letter to your baby. What have the first three months been like?

_____

_____

_____

_____

_____

_____

_____

_____

_____

_____

_____

_____

_____

_____

_____

_____

_____

_____

_____

_____

_____

Questionnaire Section

Pregnancy Sleep Risk Assessment*

You should take this quiz every four weeks during the first and third trimester starting week 4 (reminders are included on the appropriate weeks). Record your total scores in the spaces below so that you can compare your symptoms from week to week. Use the following ratings to assess your risk of falling asleep during the following activities.

0 Fully alert, no chance of falling asleep
1 Might fall asleep

2 I'm fighting to stay awake
3 It's pretty likely that I will fall asleep

If I were . . .   My chance of falling asleep is . . .

1. Talking to my partner about the pregnancy   _____

2. Driving for 30 minutes in the early afternoon   _____

3. Attending a meeting or prenatal class in the evening _____

4. Reading this journal in the afternoon   _____

5. Waiting in the car for my partner   _____

6. Watching a movie in a dark theater   _____

7. In the waiting room before an OB visit   _____

8. Getting a massage at my favorite spa   _____

9. On a short (1- to 2-hour) plane or train ride _____

10. Driving for an hour around sunset   _____

                                      Total   _____

Total your score. Here's the bottom line:

0–9   You're meeting your sleep needs   13–20 You need more sleep
10–12 You're pushing yourself a bit too hard   21–30 Without more sleep,
*Modified from the Epworth Sleepiness Scale   you're at risk of injury

DATE						
SCORE						

DATE						
SCORE						

Morning Sickness Questionnaire*

Review the numbered statements, and designate the score (0–4) that represents your answer to each question. Total your score and be sure to write down the time and date. This is your measure of your current symptom level. Repeat the questionnaire at least twice a week for as long as you have symptoms. It will help you track the severity of your symptoms, and when you're testing out treatments, allow you to measure your response to them. Talk to your doctor about treatment if your scores are high.

During the last day . . .

1. I've been nauseous:
(0) Not at all
(1) Minimally
(2) 1 or 2 episodes
(3) 3 or more episodes
(4) Continuously

2. My nausea has lasted:
(0) Not at all
(1) For an hour or less
(2) 1 or 2 hours
(3) 3 to 5 hours
(4) For 6 hours or longer

3. I have vomited:
(0) Not at all
(1) Once
(2) 2 or 3 times
(3) 4 or 5 times
(4) More than 5 times

4. Each time I vomit:
(0) N/A (I haven't)
(1) It was a small amount
(2) It was a moderate amount
(3) It was a large amount
(4) Seems to exceed what I have eaten

5. My upset stomach has:
(0) Not affected my ability to function
(1) Slowed me down a bit
(2) Moderately reduced my ability
    to function
(3) Greatly reduced my ability to function.
(4) Made me unable to eat sufficiently

* Modified from Rhodes Index of Nausea, Vomiting, and Retching

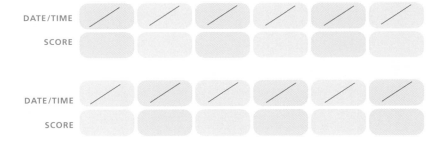

DATE/TIME

SCORE

DATE/TIME

SCORE

197

Mood Questionnaire*

Complete this questionnaire early in your pregnancy, and again every four weeks until three months after your delivery. Your answers should most accurately reflect the way that you've felt during the last week. Each time you complete the questionnaire, compare your result with your previous scores. Seek help if your scores are rising and your symptoms are getting worse.

1. I have been able to appreciate jokes and laugh at humorous situations.

(0) As much as always
(1) Not quite as much now
(2) Not much now
(3) Not at all

2. I have looked forward to what each new day will bring.

(0) As much as usual for me
(1) Somewhat less than usual for me
(2) A lot less than I used to
(3) Almost never or not at all

3. I have felt guilty when things didn't go right.

(0) I never do
(1) Hardly ever
(2) I sometimes do
(3) I often feel this way

4. I have been uncharacteristically anxious or worried.

(0) Never
(1) Hardly ever
(2) Some of the time
(3) Most of the time

5. I have felt fearful or panicked for reasons I cannot explain.

(0) I never feel this way
(1) This doesn't happen much
(2) Sometimes this happens
(3) This often happens

6. I have been feeling overwhelmed and unable to keep up.

(0) I am doing as well as ever
(1) I am coping fairly well
(2) Some of the time
(3) Most of the time

7. **I have difficulty sleeping because my mind is spinning with unhappy thoughts.**

(0) I'm not having sleep problems

(1) I'm sleeping fairly well

(2) Some nights

(3) Most nights

8. **I have been feeling sad or gloomy.**

(0) Not at all

(1) Not very often

(2) Quite often

(3) Most of the time

*Modified from the Edinburgh Postnatal Depression Scale

Total your score. Here's the bottom line:

Add the sum of your answers and record your score in the space provided below. If your score is 9 or higher, discuss your symptoms with your healthcare provider.

If you are having suicidal thoughts, contact her immediately to discuss treatment options.

DATE

SCORE

DATE

SCORE

Nutrition Questionnaire

Circle the answer that best describes your diet. Then add up your score to see how far you've come and what you still need to do to achieve the healthiest pregnancy possible.

1. Describe your weight change since the last trimester.
(0) I gained 1 to 5 pounds
(1) I gained 5.5 to 8 pounds
(2) I gained 8.5 to 10 pounds
(3) I lost weight
(4) I gained more than 10 pounds

2. What sources of protein do you typically consume each day?
(0) Nuts, grains, dairy, and eggs
(1) Dairy, eggs, or poultry
(2) Beef and poultry
(3) Beef, pork, fish and/or seafood
(4) Fish and/or seafood

3. How many servings of fruit and vegetables do you have each day?
(0) Five or more
(1) Three to four
(2) Two to three
(3) One
(4) I rarely eat fruits and vegetables

4. How do you generally feel 90 minutes after you eat dinner?
(0) Feeling just right
(1) Gassy
(2) Too full or bloated
(3) Hungry
(4) Sleepy

5. How often do you experience nausea and/or vomiting?
(0) Occasionally
(1) 1 to 2 times per week
(2) 2 to 5 times per week
(3) About once a day
(4) More than once a day

6. What are your primary sources of omega-3 fatty acids?
(0) High omega-3 foods plus 200 mg docosa-hexaenoic acid (DHA) supplement
(1) Flax oil and/or seeds, walnuts, avocado, enriched eggs
(2) Molecularly distilled fish oil
(3) Cod liver oil
(4) Fish

7. I eat organic foods . . .
(0) Almost exclusively
(1) When available
(2) Occasionally
(3) Rarely
(4) What's organic?

8. What best describes the source of fiber you consume each day?
(0) Unrefined grains and cereals, fresh fruits and/or vegetables, legumes
(1) A fiber supplement
(2) Processed foods, occasional fruit and/or vegetable
(3) Bagels, rice, and iceberg lettuce
(4) Cookies, cake, and other sweets

9. Are you certain that you get enough folic acid and other vitamins?

(0) Yes, I take a prenatal vitamin and I eat a well-rounded diet

(1) I usually take a prenatal vitamin

(2) I think so because I eat a good diet

(3) Not sure

(4) Why do I need this?

SCORE **END OF FIRST TRIMESTER**

SCORE **END OF SECOND TRIMESTER**

Total your score. Here's the bottom line:

10 or less Great! You have good eating habits, and your diet is keeping you and your baby healthy. Keep up the good work!

11-20 Not bad, but you have room for improvement. Take a moment to review the Healthy Eating for Two suggestions before proceeding. You'll fix things fast.

21-30 Time to change your ways. Your diet and eating habits are getting in your way of a healthy pregnancy. Talk to your physician about steps you can take to get your dietary habits on the right track.

31-40 Immediate call to action! Your diet and eating habits are putting your pregnancy at risk. Consider asking your healthcare provider for a referral to a licensed dietician.

Assess Your Risk for Preterm Labor

Circle the appropriate response. You will take this quiz only once, at week 26.

1. Have you experienced an episode of preterm labor before?   Yes   No

2. Are you preoccupied with worry?   Yes   No

3. Are you a tobacco user or exposed to second-hand smoke?   Yes   No

4. Have you had a LEEP cone biopsy or other surgery for abnormal Pap smear?   Yes   No

5. Are you in a high stress job?   Yes   No

6. Have you had a bladder infection during this pregnancy?   Yes   No

7. Are you pregnant with more than one baby?   Yes   No

8. Are you sedentary?   Yes   No

9. Are you dealing with this pregnancy without the support of family and friends?   Yes   No

10. Have you had an abnormal ultrasound finding earlier in your pregnancy?   Yes   No

Total Your Score: Here's the bottom line:

If you answered "yes" to more than three of these questions, you may have an increased risk of preterm labor. Talk to your doctor about whether you should have additional testing.

Aches and Pain Index*

Start taking this quiz anytime symptoms arise and return to it weekly as symptoms persist. Use the following descriptive words to answer the questions. Then add up the numbers that correspond to the descriptions for your current pain score.

1—Minimal
2—Sore
3—Distressing
4—Horrible
5—Agonizing

1. Which word describes your pain now? _____

2. Which word describes your worst day during the last week? _____

3. Which word describes the pain in your lower back? _____

4. Which word describes the pain in your pelvis/pubic bone? _____

5. Which word describes your discomfort while walking? _____

6. Which word describes your discomfort while standing? _____

Total your score. Here's the bottom line:

Document your score in the space provided below. Repeat this test at least once a week to determine if your problem is stable, better, or worse. Discuss this information with your healthcare provider when considering additional treatment.

Modified from McGill's Present Pain Index

Kick Counting

Do this activity biweekly as needed starting week 33. Plan a time when you'll have about 30 minutes each day, after a light meal or snack. Lie on your left side, with your arm across your abdomen. Count the number of times your baby moves during the half hour of monitoring. Perform this activity twice daily and record your results. Below is a chart you can use to document your fetal movement counts (photocopy it if you want to count kicks more than three times).

	THIS IS PREGNANCY WEEK NUMBER _____					
DATE						
AFTER BREAKFAST						
AFTER LUNCH						

	THIS IS PREGNANCY WEEK NUMBER _____					
DATE						
AFTER BREAKFAST						
AFTER LUNCH						

	THIS IS PREGNANCY WEEK NUMBER _____					
DATE						
AFTER BREAKFAST						
AFTER LUNCH						

How Long Until Labor?

Circle the answer that best describes you and how you have been feeling. Take it every couple of days as your due date approaches (starting week 37 and ending week 42). The results should give you an estimate of how much longer you have to wait . . .or not.

1. **What best describes your energy level over the last 48 hours?**
(0) Sluggish
(1) Calm
(2) Restless and/or agitated

2. **How have you slept the last two nights?**
(0) Slept well
(1) Woke more frequently
(2) Had insomnia

3. **How would you describe your bowel habits the last 48 hours?**
(0) Constipated
(1) Unchanged
(2) Loose and more frequent

4. **What best describes your baby's position?**
(0) About the same
(1) Lower in my abdomen
(2) Pressed against my bladder

5. **My doctor said my cervix is . . .**
(0) Unchanged
(1) Thinning
(2) Slightly dilated
(3) 1–2 cm dilated

6. **How would you describe your contractions?**
(0) Nonexistent
(1) Infrequent and go away with activity
(2) More frequent and increasing in intensity
(3) 4–5 per hour

7. **My vaginal discharge is . . .**
(0) Unchanged/nonexistent
(1) Clear or minimal
(2) Bloody or brown colored
(3) Copious and/or thicker

8. **How often have you experienced back pain over the last 48 hours?**
(0) Rarely
(1) Occasionally, but it subsides when I move
(2) Constantly, and it radiates into my lower abdomen

9. **What best describes your appetite in the last 12 hours?**
(0) Normal or increased
(1) Minimal
(2) Who can eat with all this indigestion!

10. **During this pregnancy . . .**
(0) I've had no preterm labor
(1) I've had preterm labor but did not need medication
(2) I've been on medication for preterm labor

205

Questionnaire continues on next page > > >

Total your score. Here's the bottom line.

15 or higher: Pack your overnight bag—you'll probably go into labor in the next 48 hours.

10 to 14: You probably won't deliver within the next 72 hours.

Less than 10: It's not going to happen in the next week, but just in case, don't buy any theater tickets for next weekend.

DATE

SCORE

DATE

SCORE

Post-Traumatic Stress Disorder Screening *

TAKE THIS QUESTIONNAIRE during your postpartum months if you frequently have negative thoughts or think about a back incident or if you have recurrent nightmares.

Circle yes or no for the following questions as they relate to any specific traumatic event you experienced.

1. Do you find yourself thinking about a bad incident that you'd rather forget?

Yes   No

2. Do you have recurring nightmares about your experience?

Yes   No

3. Do you ever find yourself acting as if your traumatic experience is happening again?

Yes   No

4. Does it upset you when you're reminded of the experience?

Yes   No

5. When you are reminded of the event, do you feel heart palpitations, upset stomach, dizziness, or increased sweating?

Yes   No

6. Do thoughts of your experience make it difficult for you to fall asleep or stay asleep?

Yes   No

7. Do you have angry outbursts or irritability?

Yes   No

8. Do you have difficulty concentrating or have wandering thoughts?

Yes   No

9. Do you feel hyper-vigilant or are unable to relax due to fears of harm to yourself or others you care about?

Yes   No

10. Are you easily startled?

Yes   No

TOTAL YOUR SCORE.

HERE'S THE BOTTOM LINE:
If you answered yes to six or more of the questions above, talk to your healthcare provider about seeking a diagnosis and treatment for PTSD. Though this questionnaire is not considered diagnostic, it does indicate that you meet many of the criteria associated with PTSD.

*Modified from the Trauma Screening Questionnaire.

207

Fatigue Assessment Calendar

Fill out this questionnaire every day starting at postpartum week three and continue for one month. Enter the response number that best indicates how you feel that day.

Score

0 No/never

1 Mild/occasionally

2 Moderate/frequently

3 Severe/always

		FIRST HALF OF THE MONTH													
	day 1	2	3	4	5	6	7	8	9	10	11	12	13	14	15
MONTH/ DAY															
SYMPTOM ASSESSMENT															
	SCORE														
ANXIETY															
DEPRESSION															
HEADACHE															
INCREASED APPETITE															
LOSS OF APPETITE															
PAIN															
SLEEPINESS/ DROWSINESS															
VISUAL CHANGES															
SUBTOTAL															

			FIRST HALF OF THE MONTH													
	day 1	2	3	4	5	6	7	8	9	10	11	12	13	14	15
MONTH/ DAY																
FATIGUE ASSESSMENT																
	SCORE															
I FATIGUE OR TIRE EASILY																
FATIGUE INTERFERES WITH MY ABILITY TO CARE FOR MY BABY																
FATIGUE INTERFERES WITH MY ABILITY TO CARE FOR MYSELF																
FATIGUE INTERFERES WITH MY FUNCTIONING																
FATIGUE INTERFERES WITH MY MOTIVATION																
TOTAL FOR SYMPTOM AND FATIGUE																

209

Total your score. Here's the bottom line:

This calendar is not meant to diagnose any condition, but rather to increase your awareness of your health and energy. If you find that you're not regaining your strength or if your fatigue is worsening, contact your healthcare provider and discuss tests that can rule out other causes of fatigue.

		SECOND HALF OF THE MONTH												
	day 16	17	18	19	20	21	22	23	24	25	26	27	28	29	30
MONTH/ DAY															
SYMPTOM ASSESSMENT															
	SCORE														
ANXIETY															
DEPRESSION															
HEADACHE															
INCREASED APPETITE															
LOSS OF APPETITE															
PAIN															
SLEEPINESS/ DROWSINESS															
VISUAL CHANGES															
SUBTOTAL															

210

	SECOND HALF OF THE MONTH														
	day 16	17	18	19	20	21	22	23	24	25	26	27	28	29	30
MONTH/ DAY															
FATIGUE ASSESSMENT															
	SCORE														
I FATIGUE OR TIRE EASILY															
FATIGUE INTERFERES WITH MY ABILITY TO CARE FOR MY BABY															
FATIGUE INTERFERES WITH MY ABILITY TO CARE FOR MYSELF															
FATIGUE INTERFERES WITH MY FUNCTIONING															
FATIGUE INTERFERES WITH MY MOTIVATION															
TOTAL FOR SYMPTOM AND FATIGUE															

211

Total your score. Here's the bottom line:

If you find that your fatigue is still worsening, contact your healthcare provider and discuss tests that can rule out other causes of fatigue.

Postpartum Bladder Symptom Index

Fill out this questionnaire weekly if you're experiencing frequent urination, urgency to urinate, or discomfort with sex. Add up your score and log it below to track whether your symptoms are getting better or worse. The results are valuable in deciding if you need treatment and to assess the effectiveness of any treatments you use.

1. During the last week, how often have you had a strong and sudden urge to urinate?
(0) Not at all
(1) Occasionally
(2) About once per day
(3) Several timers per day

2. Have you experienced burning, itching, pain, or pressure in your bladder?
(0) No
(1) Occasionally
(2) Frequently
(3) Continuously

3. How often do you visit the restroom between bedtime and morning?
(0) Not at all
(1) Once
(2) Twice
(3) Three or more

4. What is the typical time interval between daytime trips to the restroom?
(0) Longer than 5 hours
(1) 4 to 5 hours
(2) 3 to 4 hours
(3) Less than every 3 hours

5. Pain during sexual intercourse . . .
(0) Has not been a problem
(1) Has been a minor problem
(2) Has been a major problem
(3) Has kept us apart

6. After sexual intercourse . . .
(0) I have no pain
(1) I have continued discomfort
(2) Pain lasts for hours
(3) It takes a day or more to recover

7. During the last week, vaginal burning or itching . . .
(0) Has not been a problem
(1) Has been a minor problem
(2) Has been noticeable daily
(3) Has been severe

8. During the last week, the area around my vagina . . .
(0) Has not been sore or tender
(1) Has been somewhat sensitive
(2) Has been very raw and tender
(3) Has been very painful

Total your score. Here's the bottom line:

4 or less: You're doing pretty well. Repeat this test in a week.

5 or above: Contact your doctor to discuss your results and possible treatments and repeat test in a week.

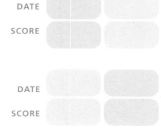

DATE

SCORE

DATE

SCORE